P9-EDS-393

COMPOSING FOR THE JAZZ ORCHESTRA

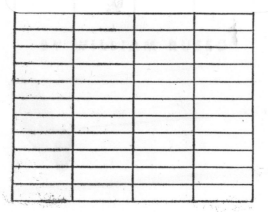

THE U   S

N

MAR 21 '88   MAR 21 '00   DEMCO

the mind feels, the heart thinks

TO MY FATHER

International Standard Book Number: 0—226—73211—8 (clothbound)
Library of Congress Catalog Card Number: 61— 8642

The University of Chicago Press, Chicago 60637
The University of Chicago Press, Ltd., London

PREFACE

The jazz orchestra is immensely important if only because it is the permanent repository of jazz; the bulk of improvising is dead or will be dead, despite tape and phonograph reproductions—in a sense, performance cannot be preserved, no matter how exquisite. But the jazz orchestra not only embraces and codifies what the jazz improviser has done. It has created a new way of looking at and combining instruments, especially brass and saxophones. It uses a chordal and melodic language which is fresh and alive. It requires from its players a dedication and spontaneity not often found in music anymore.

There are those who say that jazz cannot be written, that written jazz is a contradiction in terms. In one sense, no music can be written. Music notation has always been excruciatingly inadequate. However, the music played by Duke Ellington, Count Basie, Woody Herman, and Stan Kenton cannot be dismissed; nor can one say without perverting the reality of jazz history that the orchestra in these cases merely acts as propellent for the virtuoso soloist.

I have tried to tell the student how to use his materials. This book is not theoretical. It does not observe and classify and define. A place for such books exists, but the need for an old-fashioned practical text seems to be greater. Perhaps we have too many observers today.

On the whole, the text is drawn from my own techniques, as I first conceived them. I might add that they were pulled out of the earth, inch by inch. The text also attempts to present other techniques of jazz composition which I feel have value.

Despite all the interest in jazz at this time, there is very little opportunity for the student to get any information about its techniques. An infinitely small fraction of written jazz has been published and the jazz composer rarely accepts students.

I am actively involved in writing and performing music as this introduction is being written; I offer this work in the hope that it may answer some of the questions which so many people have asked me.

To this view this text as anything more than an extended introduction to the subject would be a mistake. I feel particularly remiss about the cavalier treatment of counterpoint and about the rudimentary approach to voicing, failings later volumes will try to correct.

I began this work in 1954. During the six years in which the book has been written and rewritten, a large number of people have contributed to its completion. Andrea Arentsen, M. Minagawa, Shirley Bentley, Lucille Butterman, Jean Wilcox, and Margaret Mikiten helped in the general job of typing and assembling the material. Lawrence Wilcox and Donald Mikiten have read portions of the manuscript. Brl Gluskin was particularly helpful in making suggestions during the beginning and formulative stages. My debt to my wife, Jeremy Warburg Russo, is enormous, not only for all the last changes and final editing which she contributed but also for the initiative and encouragement she has given me to finish the work. My greatest acknowledgment is to William Mathieu, my finest student and dear friend, who not only contributed most of the music examples but has been the best gadfly an author could wish for.

The potential of the jazz orchestra is great. It can be extended into a marvelous instrument of an alive music. I pray that this small book may somehow help.

New York, 1960   William Russo

This book was begun fifteen years ago and the idea of a new edition was at first appalling to me. After some thought (and after reading it again for the first time in ten years), however, I came to see that it might have some value, especially to the young student, even though times have changed and my second book, Jazz Composition and Orchestration (Chicago: University of Chicago Press, 1968), was intended to replace this book. Much of what I had written I have moved away from but I resisted the temptation to rewrite the book and have contented myself with relatively small changes.

Chicago, 1973   William Russo

TABLE OF CONTENTS

1	ALPHABETICAL CHORD SYMBOLS	1
2	THE SIX TYPES OF CHORDS	4
3	ELABORATION OF THE SIX TYPES OF CHORDS	6
4	BASIC HARMONIC CONSIDERATIONS	8
5	THE RANGES OF THE INSTRUMENTS	11
6	VOICING	12
7	CLOSE POSITION VOICING (I)	13
8	CLOSE POSITION VOICING (II)	15
9	CLOSE POSITION VOICING (III)	18
10	OPEN POSITION VOICING (I)	20
11	OPEN POSITION VOICING (II)	24
12	OPEN POSITION VOICING (III)	27
13	NON-CHORDAL TONES	29
14	HARMONIZATION OF NON-CHORDAL TONES (I)	31
15	HARMONIZATION OF NON-CHORDAL TONES (II)	33
16	THE THICKENED LINE	35
17	THE WIDENED LINE	36
18	PERCUSSION	37
19	THE DOUBLE BASS	41
20	THE GUITAR	45
21	THE PIANO	47
22	A PRELIMINARY VIEW OF THE ENSEMBLE	48

23   THE BASIC ENSEMBLE METHOD   49

24   THE FOUR-TONE ENSEMBLE METHOD   51

25   THE PERCUSSIVE ENSEMBLE METHOD   54

26   BRASS MUTES   56

27   THE BACKGROUND   61

28   THE PLANNING OF ORCHESTRATION   63

29   COMBINATIONS OF INSTRUMENTS   65

30   IDENTITIES   70

31   CHORDS DERIVED FROM SCALES   78

32   THE PROGRESSION OF CHORDS DERIVED FROM
     SCALES   81

33   MIXED VOICING   82

34   MIXED ENSEMBLES   86

1 ALPHABETICAL CHORD SYMBOLS

The phrase "alphabetical chord symbols" refers to a musical shorthand which is used to represent chords. It is similar to the system of Roman numeral notation used in traditional harmony except for the use of capital letters (A, B, C) rather than Roman numerals (I, II, III).

A. The alphabetical letter indicates the root tone upon which the chord is built. A letter without any number indicates a triad, which is a chord extended up to the third and fifth. Unless otherwise indicated, the third is major and the fifth is perfect.

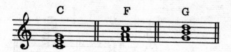

1. A minor third is indicated by the abbreviation "min."

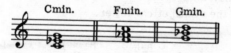

2. "+5" or (better) "#5" at the end of the symbol indicates an augmented fifth. It is best to inclose this indication in parentheses.

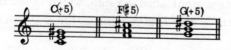

3. "-5" or (better) "♭5" at the very end of the symbol indicates a diminished fifth — also best inclosed in parentheses.

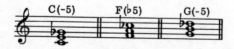

1

4.   A small circle or "dim." after the letter indicates a minor third and a diminished fifth.

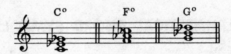

B.   The Arabic numeral "6" indicates that the major sixth is to be added to the triad. The Arabic numerals "69" indicate that <u>both</u> the sixth and the major ninth are to be added.

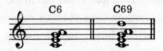

C.   The Arabic numeral "7" indicates that the minor seventh is to be added to the triad.

1.   A major seventh is indicated by "maj." or "Maj." placed after the alphabetical letter.

2.   When "7" is preceded by a small circle or by "dim.," it represents a diminished seventh, which is enharmonically a major sixth. B°7 or B dim.7 stands for B D F A♭.

D.   The Arabic numeral "9" indicates that the seventh (minor, unless major seventh is indicated) and the major ninth are to be added to the triad.

1.   A lowered ninth is indicated like this: C7 (-9) or (better) C7 (♭9).

2.   A raised ninth is indicated like this: C7 (+9) or (better) C7 (♯9).

E.   The Arabic numeral "11" indicates that the seventh (minor seventh unless major seventh is indicated), major ninth, and perfect eleventh are to be added to the triad.

A raised eleventh is indicated by a "+" preceding the "11," or as in the second example below.

F.   The Arabic numeral "13" indicates that the seventh, ninth, eleventh, and major thirteenth are to be added to the triad.

NOTE WELL: The symbols for minor affect only the third; the symbols for major affect only the seventh.

The process of naming the tones indicated by the alphabetical chord symbols is called "spelling the chord." When spelling the chord, the notes should be written on the staff. Since the alphabetical chord symbol doesn't indicate a particular octave, the chord should be spelled in the octave which will involve the least number of ledger lines above or below the staff.

The chord symbols below form a simple variation of the harmonic structure of the "blues":

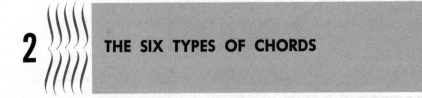

4	C69	F9	C69	G min.7	C7(♭9)
4	////	////	////	//	//

	F9	F9	C Maj.9	A7(♯9)
	////	////	////	////

	D min.9	G13(♭9)	C Maj.9	C♯o7	D min.9	D♭+11
	////	////	//	//	//	//

The vergules (/) under each chord indicate the number of beats the chord is in effect. Each vergule represents one beat of a measure.

2 THE SIX TYPES OF CHORDS

Derived from traditional harmony, the chords usually used in writing for the jazz orchestra can be classed in six groups or types. This process of classification is very important since it makes possible six sets of rules, one for each type of chord, rather than hundreds of rules for the hundreds of chords. All of the chords in one type have the same characteristics. Consequently, they can be treated in nearly the same way. This will most clearly be seen in the next chapter, which explains how tones may be added to a chord without changing its fundamental nature. In addition, knowing how to classify chords will form the basis for the process of creating harmonic progressions.

Below are the six types. The intervals referred to are from the root of the chord to each of the upper tones—not from third to fifth, fifth to seventh, etc. The measurement is always from root to third, root to fifth, root to seventh, etc.

MAJOR TYPE CHORD: a chord having all major and perfect intervals.

MINOR TYPE CHORD: a chord having all major and perfect intervals except for the third, which is minor.

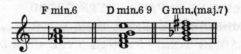

MINOR SEVENTH TYPE CHORD: a chord having all major and perfect intervals except for the third and seventh, which are minor.

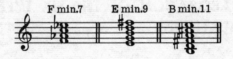

DOMINANT SEVENTH TYPE CHORD: a chord having a major third and a minor seventh.

(An augmented triad is also a DOMINANT SEVENTH TYPE CHORD as is a triad with major third and diminished fifth.

DIMINISHED SEVENTH TYPE CHORD: a chord having a minor third and a diminished fifth.

LEADING TONE SEVENTH TYPE CHORD: a chord having a minor third, diminished fifth, and a minor seventh.

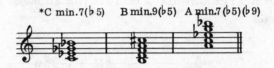

These are the abbreviations for the six types of chords:

MAJOR TYPE CHORD	MAJ
MINOR TYPE CHORD	MIN
MINOR SEVENTH TYPE CHORD	MS
DOMINANT SEVENTH TYPE CHORD	DS
DIMINISHED SEVENTH TYPE CHORD	DIM
LEADING TONE SEVENTH TYPE CHORD	LTS

3   ELABORATION OF THE SIX TYPES OF CHORDS

This chapter will deal with the adding of tones to the various chords— tones which will not alter the nature of the chord. These added tones may be used melodically or harmonically.

The previous chapter makes possible the treatment of chords as groups rather than as countless individual structures. Below are six sets of rules governing the additions to and alterations of the six chord types.

*Today (1973) the more common alphabetical designation for these three chords is   Cø7   Bø7(9)   Aø7(♭9)

TYPE OF CHORD	ADDITIONS OR ALTERATIONS
MAJ	a major 6th, major 7th, major 9th

| MIN | a major 6th, major 7th, major 9th, perfect 11th |

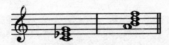

| MS | a major 9th, perfect 11th |

| DS | a major 9th, perfect 11th, major 13th; the 5th may be raised or lowered, the 9th may be raised or lowered, the 11th may be raised (the raised 11th is usually preferred on DS type chords) |

| DIM | a major 7th, major 9th, perfect 11th, minor 13th |

| LTS | a major 9th, perfect 11th, minor 13th; the 9th may be lowered |

It is not necessary or desirable to use <u>all</u> additional or altered tones at the same time. Harmonically (that is, simultaneously), it is especially undesirable to use the altered form of a chord tone with the unaltered form, although using both the lowered and raised form of a chord tone is permissible.

Harmonically, the ninth is usually not added without the sixth or seventh; the eleventh is usually not added without the sixth or seventh and ninth—but this is by no means a requirement.

4 BASIC HARMONIC CONSIDERATIONS

The "arranging" of popular or standard tunes has been a basic part of the jazz composer's training and work, though this process could better be called "re-composition." The application of the material in this lesson will simplify and clarify the basic harmonic structures of such tunes and will greatly facilitiate their artistic treatment. It is much simpler to begin the melodic, orchestral, and harmonic changes involved in the re-composition of a piece after its chords have been trimmed and are clearly understood.

When working with lead sheets or piano sheets, three things should be taken into consideration: the alphabetical chord symbols, the melody, and the actual notes of the accompaniment. There are often mistakes and omissions in the printing of the chord symbols and a study of the melody and accompaniment may correct these before the following process is applied.

A.   Diatonic chords move freely among themselves. That is, any diatonic chord may progress to any other diatonic chord. (The material covered in chap. 13 deals further with "standard" chordal progressions.)

B.   It is often difficult to distinguish between a MIN and an MS because there is a certain amount of interchangeability between the two. They are identical triads, with the addition of the major sixth or minor seventh forming the distinction. Often, the difference that does exist between them is not preserved in lead sheets or piano copies. Some aids to the distinction are: (1) most often, if the chord progresses to a DS a perfect fourth above or a minor second below, it is an MS; (2) most often, if the chord progresses to a DS a major second above or a major third below, it is a MIN; (3) if the major sixth would be diatonic to the key or tonality, it is most likely a MIN; (4) if the minor seventh would be diatonic to the key or the tonality, it is most likely an MS (in the key of C, for example, E min. would more <u>likely</u> be an MS than a MIN); (5) if the chord sets up a new tonality, it is more likely a MIN.

C. As between the MS and the MIN, the first three tones of the chord do not distinguish the DIM from the LTS. In this case, though, the diminished triad almost always refers to the DIM, not to the LTS.

D. A diminished chord may be derived from any DS type chord. Adding the lowered ninth and omitting the root produces a diminished seventh chord built on the third. This point is more significant when reversed: most diminished seventh chords are derived from a DS; they can be better understood by finding this DS. There are only three diminished seventh chords (CE♭G♭A; FA♭C♭D, B♭D♭F♭G)—all others being enharmonically the same. Thus, one diminished seventh chord can be related to four DS's.

E. A DIM built on the I of the key or tonality is usually not related to a DS, especially in progressions like this:

C MAJOR   C   Co7   Dmin.7.

F. It is best to consolidate different forms of the same chord. For example, the succession of C7(♭9), C9, C7(♭5), is best thought of as C7.

G. With a DS type chord the altered ninth is usually preferable when the chord resolves to a MIN, MS, or LTS type chord built a perfect fourth above. The thirteenth is more often used when the ninth is not altered.

H. The DS type chord built on the fourth degree of the key (F7 in the key of C) and the DS type chord built on the second degree of the key (D7 in the key of C) are usually best treated without alteration of fifth or ninth, although the raised eleventh is good. This applies to the F7 when treated like this: C F7 C; to the D7 when treated like this: C D7

Dmin.7 or C Dmin.7 D7 C. The F7 in this case is really the subdominant chord with a minor seventh added. It is, then, a MAJ although it has characteristics of the DS, too.

I.   With the exception of the two DS type chords mentioned in paragraph H above, any DS type chord can be replaced by another DS type chord built on the tone an augmented fourth below. For a C7, then, a G♭7 could be substituted. For a B7, an F7 could be substituted.

J.   A DS with a raised fifth usually rejects the altered ninth. If the ninth is added, it is more frequently unaltered. Also, a DS with a raised fifth is most suitable for the substitution referred to in paragraph I, above.

K.   Following is a table of cadences essentially representing the progression of G7 to a chord built on C. The entire table can be transposed to the eleven other DS's.

Columns X and Y represent the G7, which creates the "pushing" motion. Column Y is the "master" chord and X is the "helper." Column Z is the resolution or point of repose.

Column Y progresses directly into Column Z. The combination of Columns X and Y sometimes does not progress into Column Z at all but continues to move, often into another combination of X and Y.

COLUMN X	COLUMN Y	COLUMN Z
Usually at the beginning of the measure or group of measures	Usually at the end of the measure or group of measures	As with X, usually at the beginning of the measure or group of measures
Dmin.7 (to any chord in Y)	G7 (to any chord in Z)	C (Emin.7 Amin.7)
Dmin. (to any chord in Y)	D♭7 (to any chord in Z)	Cmin.
		Cmin.7
F (to any chord in Y)	B♭9 (to first 3 chords in Z)	Cmin.7 (♭5)
Fmin. (to first 4 chords in Y)	Fmin.7 (to any chord in Z)	rarely: Co7 C7
Dmin.7(♭5) (to first 4 chords in Y)	Fmin. (to any chord in Z)	
Fmin.7 (to first 3 chords in Y)	Co7 (to first chord in Z)	
A♭ (to first 2 chords in Y)		
A♭min. (to first 2 chords in Y)		
A♭min.7 (to first 2 chords in Y)		

5 THE RANGES OF THE INSTRUMENTS

Without exception, wind instruments present great difficulties in the extremes of their ranges. Not only are tones in the extremes difficult to
produce (especially in the upper register for the brass instruments),
but maneuverability is greatly limited.

Many jazz orchestras have exhibited a great deal of virtuosity, both
of soloists and as a group. This virtuosity is to be commended but should
not be expected or anticipated.

Non-wind instruments have an infinitely high technical potential. The
players of these instruments in the jazz orchestra, however, are often
very limited—technically and in general musicianship. Consequently,
the parts for these instruments should be very simple.

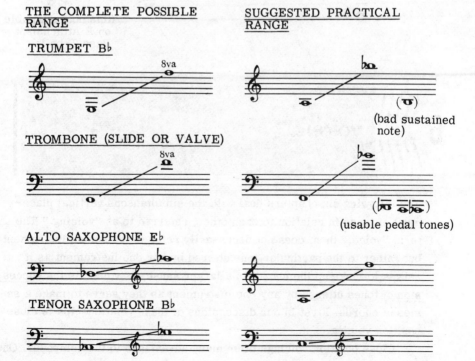

THE COMPLETE POSSIBLE
RANGE

SUGGESTED PRACTICAL
RANGE

TRUMPET B♭

(bad sustained
note)

TROMBONE (SLIDE OR VALVE)

(usable pedal tones)

ALTO SAXOPHONE E♭

TENOR SAXOPHONE B♭

BARITONE SAXOPHONE E♭

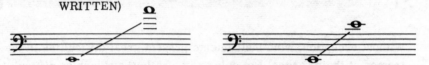

DOUBLE BASS (ALWAYS SOUNDS AN OCTAVE LOWER THAN WRITTEN)

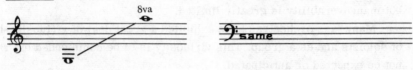

GUITAR (ALWAYS SOUNDS AN OCTAVE LOWER THAN WRITTEN)

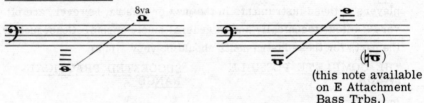

BASS TROMBONE

(this note available on E Attachment Bass Trbs.)

6 VOICING

The following six chapters deal with the simultaneous vertical placement of tones in relation to each other, referred to as "voicing." The term "voice," then, does not necessarily refer to the human instrument but rather to the particular tone uttered by any one instrument as it serves to make up the chord. In a larger sense, a "voice" is the succession of tones uttered by any one instrument as they serve to make a series of chords. First in our discussions of these relationships is close position voicing.

Close position voicings offer many advantages to the composer. One of the most important is the flow and sweep of combined melody and harmony.

The considerations for open position voicings are similar to those in close position voicings. Where close position voicings give sweep and flow, open position voicings are anchored and full. Close position voicing is often parallelistic. Open position voicing is usually interwoven and textured.

To make possible a discussion of the theoretical aspects of voicing without the intrusion of orchestral considerations, specific instruments will not be referred to at first.

7 CLOSE POSITION VOICING (I)

Following are some elementary ideas about close position voicing. At first the melody tone will be supported by tones from the chord, assigned in a downward process. The voices so formed, even the bottom or bass voice, will have little melodic importance and will often be disorderly. After the preliminaries have been dealt with, an attempt will be made to give the bass voice a melodic quality and a meaningful relationship to the lead voice. Later, techniques of smoothing out the inner voices will be discussed. The ultimate aim of achieving melodic sense in each voice and a sensible relationship between all the voices is beyond the scope of this volume.

A.   The thirteenth, eleventh, ninth, or major seventh may be used only in the lead or melody voice or beneath a higher extension (a ninth may be used beneath an eleventh, for example).

This serves to limit the tones that may be added to the particular chord in question. For example: If the lead or melody note is C and the chord is C, even though A, B, and D may be added to the chord without changing its fundamental character, only the A may be added with this lead tone. The use of the two other tones would be a violation.

B.   After it has been determined which tones may be added to the chord in question, all the tones should be placed directly beneath the lead or melody tone. These tones should be as close together as possible. It should not be possible to insert any of the available tones between any of the voices.

C.   With a thirteenth, eleventh, ninth, or major seventh in the lead voice, an "inverted" root position is to be used. That is, the voicing will go down in the order in which the chord was built. The term "inverted" root position is used since it is possible, depending on the number of voices and the number of tones in the chord, that the root may not be in the lowest voice. A C min.11 with an F in the lead would be voiced from the top down like this:

D.   A thirteenth, eleventh, ninth, or major seventh should not be doubled. These tones should be used once only—as they first appear in an upper voice.

Here are two illustrations of paragraphs A, B, C, and D: (1) Dmin. with an A in the lead or melody. This is a MIN; B, C♯, E, and G can be added to it. Since the fifth of the chord is in the lead, the C♯, E, and G cannot be added here. Only the B may be added. The chord would be voiced:

(2) Dmin. with a G in the lead or melody. In this case, all the possible tones may be used. The chord would be voiced in inverted root position.

The perfect eleventh, major ninth, and major seventh would be used only at the top of the voicing.

Although both the major seventh and major sixth may be used here, placing them next to each other requires caution.

It would be better to use them separately like this:

The extensions should be used in upper voices only since they tend to become muddy in the middle and lower voices. Also, they have too much ring and vitality to be used more than once.

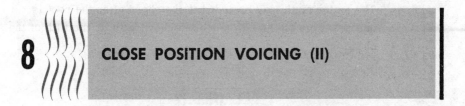

8 CLOSE POSITION VOICING (II)

A.   A DS (dominant seventh type chord) is traditionally the most powerful of the chords. It is the chord which keeps the harmonic stream flowing. At the same time it binds all the chords together.

A plain dominant seventh chord (root, third, unaltered fifth, and minor seventh) fulfils this function when the chords of other types are simple triads. Among fuller harmonic structures, however, a plain dominant seventh chord is generally weak.

The plain dominant seventh chord can be avoided in these ways:

1.   The substitute DS may be used. This is the DS built on the tone an augmented fourth below the root of the original chord (see chap. 4). This is valuable only if the substitution will make the

lead tone richer in relationship to the new chord.

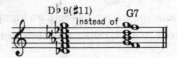

2. The fifth may be raised or lowered.

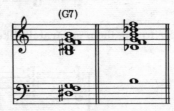

3. The derived diminished seventh chord may be used. (This chord is built on the third of a DS; the lowered ninth is added to the chord; the root is omitted [see chap. 4, paragraph D].)

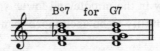

4. The major ninth may be added to the chord after the root is omitted. This forms a minor sixth chord built on the fifth of the chord.

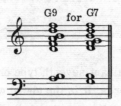

B. Some further modifications of this material may be made for larger numbers of voices, especially when the passages involved are slow-moving and/or sustained.

   1. The lowest voice may pass over a possible chordal tone, dropping down one notch to the next available chordal tone.

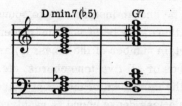

2.   The root of a DS, LTS, DIM may be treated as the fifteenth.

3.   The third of any chord may be treated as the tenth. The ninth may be used directly beneath only if no minor second between adjacent voices will result.

4.   The fifth of any chord may be treated as the twelfth. The same injunction against minor seconds in adjacent voices holds here.

9   CLOSE POSITION VOICING (III)

A.   At times it may be necessary to omit tones from chords. First, there may not be enough instruments to sound all the tones in the chord. Second, while there may be enough instruments, it may be desirable to use only a certain number of the tones: (a) as a method of preserving all four-tone chords or all five-tone chords, etc., or (b) to make possible variations in the movement of the lower voices (see paragraph C, below), or (c) because a less dense chord is required by the context.

1.   Either the fifth or root of a chord may be omitted. It is gener-ally not wise to omit both at the same time. Leaving out the fifth disturbs the quality of the chord least.

2.   The third is the tone which usually defines the quality of the chord. It should never be omitted.

3.   The minor seventh of a chord should never be omitted.

4.   The thirteenth may be treated as the added sixth. Thus the elev-enth or the eleventh and the ninth may be omitted. In this case, the fifth or the root may also be omitted.

5.   The eleventh of a MIN, MS, LTS, or DIM may be treated as the added fourth. Thus the ninth may be omitted. In this case, the fifth or the root may also be omitted. NOTE WELL: Neither the added sixth nor the added fourth should be doubled.

B.   The main characteristic of close position voicing is a number of voices which more or less exactly follow the melody line. In its most severe and extreme form this concept is responsible for the "thickened line" and the "widened line" (see chaps. 16 and 17).

The parallel approximation of a melody line is in direct contrast to the methods of open position voicing, in which parallel motion is excep-tional and the melodic flow of each voice is carefully considered. How-ever, there are certain principles of open position writing which can be applied to all close position writing except for the forms of the thickened line.

1.   The seventh should usually progress down a tone.

2.   An altered tone usually progresses in the direction of its alteration. (A lowered tone, for example, usually moves downward.)

3.   Harmony parts should not make skips much larger than the
lead (except possibly the lowest part).

4.   The skip of the augmented fourth and, to a lesser extent, the
skip of a diminished fifth should be avoided (unless the skip of
an augmented fourth is followed by a minor second step in the
same direction or the skip of a diminished fifth is followed by
a minor second step in the opposite direction).

The above four rules do not apply to changes from one position to
another of the same chord.

C.   The movement of the lower voices can be altered in these ways
(in accordance with the ideas of paragraphs B and D):

1.   Through selection of a different tone for the lead when this is
possible. (The melody may be changed or, more likely, the
lead note of the background may be changed.)

2.   Through use of a substitute or added chord.

3.   Through alteration, when possible.

4. Through treating the lead tone in different ways (as fifth instead of twelfth, twelfth instead of fifth, etc.).

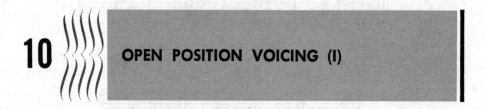

D. The lowest voice in larger groups of instruments should begin to assume a melodic entity. This can be accomplished by the manipulation suggested above or by dropping the lowest part to the next available chordal tone.

10 OPEN POSITION VOICING (I)

The Arabic numerals below (on page 23) represent the open distribution of tones of the chord. They are to be read from bottom to top, as they would appear on the staffs. The first column, then, would represent the following tones for a C chord.

These positions can be used for any five instruments. They are well suited to five saxophones (two altos, two tenors, and baritone) or five trombones. They can be used for mixed groups of instruments such as (from the top down) trumpet, alto saxophone, trombone, tenor saxophone, and baritone saxophone. They are not as useful in the upper registers. (They are best when the lead note is below d^2 in the treble clef.)

The primary use of open position chords is to form a sustained background. They may also be used as a harmonization of a melody, although there are not enough positions shown in this chapter to make this possible.

A.   Tones in common between two chords should be held over by the same voice when possible. This rule applies especially to the inner voices and to the more basic tones of the chord.

B.   The seventh of a chord moving to another chord built on the tone a perfect fourth above (i.e., C7 to F7) should resolve to the third of the new chord.

An exception to this would involve a progression in which the seventh of the first chord is major and the third of the second chord is minor.

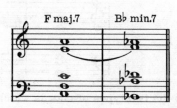

Generally, the seventh of <u>any</u> chord should resolve down a major second or a minor second.

When two voices have the seventh, only one of the two is bound by this rule.

C.   Skips of more than a major third by the inner voices are prohibited. The bottom voice may make skips of not more than an octave. The lead voice may make skips of not more than a perfect fifth.

D.   Contrary and/or oblique motion is desirable.

Between chords whose roots are adjoining, parallel motion (in the direction of the roots) is natural and <u>may</u> be preferable.

E.   With the two types of chords which permit alteration, the numerals in the columns below may be correspondingly changed.

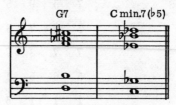

POSITIONS (read from top to bottom)

MAJOR AND MINOR
TYPE CHORDS

9	9	3	7	3	7	6
6	7	7	3	7	3	3
3	3	3	7	5	5	5
5	5	5	5	1	1	1
1	1	1	1	5	5	5

MINOR SEVENTH TYPE
CHORDS

9	5	3	7	1	7	3	5	7	7	3
7	3	7	3	5	5	5	3	3	3	7
4	7	3	7	3	3	3	7	7	5	5
5	5	5	5	7	7	7	1	1	1	1
1	1	1	1	1	1	1	5	5	11	11

DOMINANT SEVENTH
TYPE CHORDS

9	9	9	1	13	11
7	13	5	13	3	9
3	3	3	3	7	7
5	7	7	7	5	3
1	1	1	1	1	5
9	13	11	3	13	11
7	9	9	13	3	7
3	7	3	3	7	3
1	3	7	7	1	5
5	5	1	1	5	1

LEADING TONE SEVENTH TYPE CHORDS				
7	5	9	5	3
3	3	7	3	7
7	7	3	7	5
5	5	5	1	1
1	1	1	5	5

DIMINISHED SEVENTH TYPE CHORDS			
6	9	6	7
3	6	3	3
1	3	6	6
5	5	1	5
1	1	5	1

11 OPEN POSITION VOICING (II)

In the previous chapter, the basic principles of open position voicing were outlined. These principles were applied to writing for five voices; they can also be applied to writing for four voices and six voices.

A.   The positions below can be applied most naturally to four saxophones (preferably alto, two tenors, and baritone) or to four trombones. They can also be used for mixed groups of instruments such as (from the top down) trumpet, alto, trombone, alto saxophone, trombone, baritone saxophone.

POSITIONS (read from top to bottom)

MAJOR AND MINOR TYPE CHORDS							
3	7	6	7	7	3	5	9
7	3	3	3	3	6	9	6
5	5	5	6	1	1	6	10
1	1	1	1	5	5	3	1

MINOR SEVENTH TYPE CHORDS					
5	7	7	9	3	
3	3	3	5	7	
7	5	1	7	5	
1	1	5	3	1	

DOMINANT SEVENTH TYPE CHORDS					
13	13	3	5	11	9
3	9	9	9	3	13
7	7	7	7	7	3
1	3	1	3	1	7

LEADING TONE SEVENTH TYPE CHORDS		
3	7	3
7	3	7
5	5	1
1	1	5

DIMINISHED SEVENTH TYPE CHORDS		
3	5	7
6	3	3
5	6	6
1	1	1

B. The positions below can best be applied to six saxophones (two alto saxophones, three tenor saxophones, baritone saxophone) or to six brass (three trumpets and three trombones).

POSITIONS (read from top to bottom)

MAJOR AND MINOR TYPE CHORDS					
9	6	7	7	9	5
6	3	5	3	6	9
3	1	3	7	3	6
1	5	7	5	7	3
5	1	5	1	5	5
1	5	1	5	1	1

MINOR SEVENTH TYPE CHORDS

9	9	5	11	5	9
7	7	9	9	3	7
3	3	7	7	7	3
7	7	3	3	5	5
5	1	5	5	1	1
1	5	1	1	11	11

DOMINANT SEVENTH TYPE CHORDS

9	9	5	11	13	13
5	7	9	9	3	9
3	3	13	7	9	7
7	1	3	3	7	3
5	5	7	5	1	1
1	1	1	1	5	5

LEADING TONE SEVENTH TYPE CHORDS

7	9	11	5	13	13
5	7	9	9	3	9
3	3	13	7	9	7
7	1	3	3	7	3
5	5	5	1	1	1
1	1	1	5	5	5

DIMINISHED SEVENTH TYPE CHORDS

11	9	9	9	13
9	6	13	7	9
6	3	3	5	6
3	1	6	1	3
5	5	5	6	1
1	1	1	3	5

12   OPEN POSITION VOICING (III)

The positions from the lists included in the two previous chapters on open position voicing should be used by the student until he completely masters them. Ultimately, he should derive positions from the process presented below. Some of the positions so derived may coincide with those from the lists, which were evolved over many years by many people and are durable and useful.

The process of forming new positions is outlined below. At first, new positions should only be used between positions from the lists. The new positions should have the characteristics of those contained within the lists. To a certain extent, they should be formed by the melodic inclination of the individual voices.

A.   The voices should form a roughly equal distribution from each other. There is a tendency to have slightly larger intervals between the lower voices than between the upper voices. Particularly to be avoided is the combined use of smaller and larger intervals between the voices, especially contrary to the aforementioned tendency (unless required by the melodic inclination of the individual voices).

B.   An altered tone (in relationship to the key or tonality) should proceed in the direction of its alteration. A raised tone usually rises and a lowered tone usually descends, both by stepwise motion (motion of a major or minor second).

C.   Progression of the individual voices: Stepwise motion is usually good; skips of a major or minor third are good; skips of a perfect fourth or fifth are usually good. Major and minor sixth skips are good, although too large for the inner voices. The augmented fourth or diminished fifth can be the least melodic interval for any voice. It is too large a skip for the inner voices; it can be awkward for the outer voices. When the augmented fourth is used, it should be followed by a minor second in the same direction. When a diminished fifth is used, it should be followed by a minor second in the opposite direction. Intervals of a seventh or larger tend to disrupt the continued quality of the open position sound.

D.   As mentioned in paragraph A of chapter 9, certain tones can be omitted from chords. The rules governing the omission of tones are applicable to the material in this chapter.

E.   Less usual tones may be used in the lower voice of the positions under these conditions: first, that the chord progressions involved are clear and expected; second, that the chord in question is fairly simple; third, that a better melodic flow of the lowest voice is obtained; fourth, that the root of the chord is maintained.

F.   Parallel motion between chords of the same type, especially when they are in the same form (with the same added tones) and in the same position, is quite acceptable. The forward push of the parallelism is minimized by the similarity of the chords, relieving the worst aspects of parallelism.

G.   Parallel motion between chords of different types which are in the same position is sometimes quite satisfactory. For example, an F chord in 1 5 3 6 9 position can move in parallel motion up to a B♭7 in 1 5 3 7 9 position. (The difference of position between the seventh of one chord and the sixth of the other is irrelevant.)

H.   Except for the deliberate parallelism of paragraphs F and G, above, an octave between any two voices should not be led into by similar motion. In other words, no two voices should move into an octave from the same direction (either above or below). Too much attention is directed to an octave so approached, detracting from the flow of the harmony. But such parallelism is quite acceptable at a point of repose.

I.   Each group of open position voicings will form a phrase even if used as an accompaniment. A single phrase is often played in one breath; in fact, it often corresponds to the limit of one breath—that is, the length of a single phrase is connected with the breathing capacity of the player. Each phrase should be complete within itself except the first phrase of a two-phrase group; such a phrase may rely on the second phrase for completion.

J.   The rules of voicing are less strict between the last chord of one phrase and the first chord of a following phrase. When two phrases are sufficiently separated so that each is defined from the other, there is no obligation to follow any voicing procedure between them.

K.   The use of an identity (see chap. 30) between voicings (either open or close voicings) eliminates in direct proportion to the length of the identity, the need for voice-leading between the last chord preceding the identity and the first chord following it: the longer the identity the less attention need be paid to voice-leading.

13 NON-CHORDAL TONES

A chordal tone is: (a) a tone within the basic chord; (b) a tone that can be added to the basic chord; or (c) the alteration of either a basic tone or an added tone. A non-chordal tone is any tone that cannot be classified as (a), (b), or (c) in relationship to the chord in question. A non-chordal tone is, then, any tone not basically or potentially in the chord.

There are two classes of non-chordal tones:

A.   Non-chordal tones which are attached to or related to following and/or preceding chordal tones:

1.   PASSING TONES: a tone or tones connecting two different but adjoining chordal tones chromatically or diatonically.

2.   NEIGHBORING TONES: a tone or tones chromatically or diatonically leading into a chordal tone—from a skip or preceded by a rest.

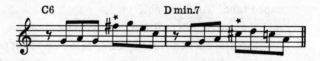

3.   AUXILIARY TONES: a tone or tones connecting the same chordal tone chromatically or diatonically.

4. CHANGING TONES: tones leading chromatically or diatonically into a chordal tone from above and below (or below and
above).

B. Non-chordal tones which are attached only to preceding chordal tones or which are not attached to chordal tones at all:

1. REVERSED NEIGHBORING TONES: a tone or tones chromatically or diatonically proceeding <u>from</u> a chordal tone to a skip.

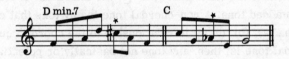

2. ESCAPED TONES: a tone or tones which have, as the name
implies, escaped from the chord; an escaped tone is not connected, either before or after, to a chordal tone.

3. BLUE NOTES: unusual alterations (which can almost be considered "distortions") of chordal tones; to be considered a
blue note, the tone must not be attached to either a following
or preceding chordal tone; it is a particular form of an escaped tone. The blue note is:

(a) the minor third of MAJ or DS type chords
(b) the diminished fifth of MAJ, MIN, or MS type chords
(c) the minor seventh of MAJ or MIN type chords
(d) the minor sixth of MAJ, MIN, or MS type chords

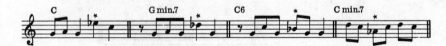

14

HARMONIZATION OF NON-CHORDAL TONES (I)

When non-chordal tones are contained in a single tone line, they present no technical problem. When they occur within a passage that is being voiced, however, they must be harmonized. A non-chordal tone of importance (greater time value, prominent position, accent) will tend to change the harmonic nature of the original chord. When the non-chordal tone is of less importance, it can be "accommodated" within the basic harmony; it will change the basic harmonic scheme very little.

The harmonizations below are for the less important non-chordal tones. This list contains many of the best harmonizations. Some are often used and some are found infrequently. Those at the beginning of each group are more common.

TYPE OF CHORD	HARMONIZATION
MAJ	(a) a DIM built a minor second below the root of the chord in question
	(b) a LTS built a minor second below the root of the chord in question
	(c) a MS or MIN built a perfect fourth above the root of the chord in question
	(d) a LTS or MS built a major second below the root of the chord in question
	(e) a DIM built on the tone in question
	(f) any chord of the same type*
MIN	(a) a MIN or MS built a perfect fourth above the root of the chord in question
	(b) a DIM built a minor second below the root of the chord in question

---
*especially a minor second or a major second above or below.

(c) a LTS built a major second below the root
of the chord in question

(d) a DIM built on the tone in question

(e) any chord of the same type*

(f) a MAJ built a minor second above the root
of the chord in question

MS   (a) a MIN or MS built a perfect fourth above
the root of the chord in question

(b) a DIM built a minor second below the root
of the chord in question

(c) a DIM built on the tone in question

(d) any chord of the same type*

(e) a MAJ built a minor second above the root
of the chord in question

DS   The major seventh is the only actual non-
chordal tone of this chord. The perfect eleventh
is almost always treated as a non-chordal tone,
though.

(a) a MS built a perfect fifth above the root of
the chord in question

(b) a MAJ, MIN, or MS built a perfect fourth
above the root of the chord in question

(c) a DIM built on the tone in question

(d) any chord of the same type*

DIM   This chord may be related to a DS (see chap. 4,
paragraph D and E). If so, the tone should be
treated in relationship to it. If not:

(a) the chord following the chord in question

(b) any chord of the same type*

LTS   (a) a DIM built a minor second below the root
of the chord in question

(b) a DIM built on the tone in question

(c) any chord of the same type*

---

*especially a minor second or a major second above or below.

A non-chordal tone which coincides with the beginning of its accompanying chord must be harmonized very carefully. The harmonization used for such a tone must also relate (in terms of the list above) to the previous chord.

A non-chordal tone which coincides with the end of its accompanying chord would be treated similarly. In this case the chord used for such a tone must relate to the following chord also.

15 HARMONIZATION OF NON-CHORDAL TONES (II)

It is sometimes desirable to treat a chordal tone as a non-chordal tone.

A.   There are two reasons for treating a chordal tone as a non-chordal tone:

1.   To enrich an harmonically dull passage; the use of the same chord for different melody tones can be very awkward (more so, in fact, than if the chord is sustained for the same length of time).

2.   To obtain all four-tone chords, which is very important to certain types of close position voicing. (A chordal tone may be treated as a non-chordal tone so that all five-tone or all six-tone chords may be derived, also. This is not immediately pertinent, however.)

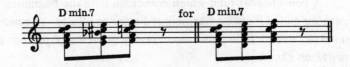

B.   The tone in question must fulfil these qualifications before being treated as a non-chordal tone:

1.   It must be followed by a tone a minor or major second away. (This tone is usually a chord tone or a tone resolving—by a sec-one—into a chord tone.)

2.   It must be a less important tone. That is, it must exist primarily in relationship to another tone. It should have less value than a beat; it should less frequently fall on the downbeat; it should be an unaccented tone; it should be a lower tone—both in relationship to the preceding and following tones and in relationship to the phrase as a whole. (It is more likely that a less basic chordal tone will be treated as a non-chordal tone than a basic chordal tone; e.g., the ninth is more likely to be treated as a non-chordal tone than the third.)

The following list contains some chords that can be used for chordal tones treated as non-chordal tones. These chords are an addition to the list contained in the previous chapter.

TYPE OF CHORD	POSSIBLE HARMONIZATION
MAJ	a MS built a major third above the root of the chord in question
MIN	a DS (without alteration of the ninth) built a perfect fourth above the root of chord in question
MS	(a) a MS built a perfect fourth above the root of the chord in question
	(b) a DS (without alteration of the ninth) built a perfect fourth above the root of the chord in question
DS	(a) a MIN built a minor second above the root of the chord in question
	(b) a MIN or LTS built a perfect fifth above the root of chord in question

For a more prominent non-chordal tone (or chordal tone being treated as a non-chordal tone), it is better to use a harmonization which (a) contains some tones of the original chord, or (b) is closely related to the original chord (the DIM a minor second below or the DS a perfect fourth below).

16   THE THICKENED LINE

The thickened line is just what its name implies: the filling out or thickening of a melodic line. It is a <u>form</u> of close position voicing.

It is here that all the material on harmonization of non-chordal tones will be used. The thickened line differs from general close position voicing in these respects:

1.   All four-tone chords must be used.

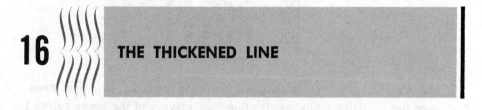

2.   Each of the lower voices must move in approximation of the contour of the lead line—moving up when the lead line moves up, moving down when the lead line moves down, and remaining on the same tone when the lead line remains on the same tone (unless the chord changes and the lead tone repeats).

3.   If there are more than four instruments used, they must exactly double the four voices. If the first voice is doubled an octave lower, minor seconds may result between it and the fourth voice. This is permissible.

4.   When a larger chord is suggested by the lead tone (a ninth, or eleventh, for example), only four tones <u>from</u> it may be used (see chap. 9, paragraph A).

The thickened line is designed for rapid passages. It is best when used for solo-like melodies. It allows the players of the lower voices to duplicate the lead voice in highly individualized and subtle interpretative techniques—the identical contours of all four voices make identical stress and accent and inflection easier to achieve.

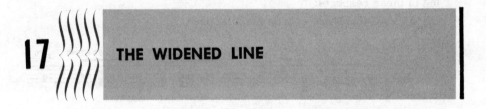

17   THE WIDENED LINE

The thickened line consists of the lead or melody line and three harmony voices. It may be desirable to "widen" the thickened line. This can be very effectively done by dropping one or more of the voices down an octave. For example, the second voice could be dropped an octave, the third and fourth voices remaining in their original octaves.

The main consideration when dropping voices is that the resultant distribution must be proportional. The lead voice, if set a large inter-val above three voices crowded together, would weaken the homogene-ous quality of the close position sound. The ear would be aware of sep-arate voices; it should be led to hear an amplified single line.

It is best if the adjoining voices in the widened line contain the least number of seconds between them. (In all uses of the thickened line the student should write out the basic four voices, each on a separate staff, so that he will be able to make a further disposition of the parts.)

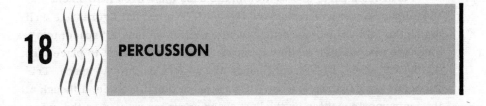

18   PERCUSSION

The aim of this material on the percussion instruments is threefold: (a) to illustrate the best of the tradition of jazz drums; (b) to suggest ways in which the tradition can be expanded; and (c) to make the part played by the drums less subject to the aesthetics and abilities of the drummer and more under the control of the composer.

The drum part today is a guide for the player. It should and can contain more frequent written passages. At first, the student should use the simplified approach which is generally practiced, gradually moving toward more expressive and defined percussion writing.

The percussion instruments which have an important place within the jazz orchestra are snare drum; bass drum; single cymbal; double, attached, cymbals (the "hi-hat"); tom-tom; triangle; tympani; and gong. To this list can be added the entire group of instruments which are es-sentially used for Latin-American or Afro-Cuban music. This group will not be dealt with in this book (see Morales and Adler, Latin-American Rhythm Instruments and How To Play Them, [New York: Kar-Val Pub-lishing Corp., 1949]).

There are three main subsidiary percussive implements: sticks, mallets (sticks with padded ends), and brushes (consisting of a short handle from which spring 20 to 40 wires, each about five inches long).

The percussion instruments in the jazz orchestra are usually played by one musician. They form what is called the drum set. In minimum form, the set consists of snare drum, bass drum (played with the right foot by means of a foot pedal), 2 single cymbals (suspended above the bass drum on metal rods), and hi-hat. The distance between the two cymbals of the hi-hat is controlled by the left foot—the hi-hat can be made to sound with the foot control alone.

The snare is played with sticks or brushes. The single cymbals are played with sticks, brushes, or mallets. The hi-hat is usually played by sticks but sometimes by brushes (most often in conjunction with the foot control). The use of mallets on the hi-hat should be avoided.

Percussion parts are written in the bass clef. Each instrument should have a particular place on the staff. The cymbal figures are written on the "G" space; snare figures are written on the "E" space; tom-toms are also written on the "E" space, although it is best to place them on the "C" space; bass drum figures are written on the "A" space. Triangle and gong figures are usually written on the "G" space, although all the instruments written on the "G" space are often written on the space above the staff. Since placement is not standardized, it is best to specify the particular instrument at each new entrance.

On fast pieces, the bass drum plays quarter notes very lightly—but only in conjunction with the 4/4 double bass line. This reinforces the double bass line almost inaudibly, although its absence would be noticeable.

Using sticks, it is conventional for the drummer to play some form of

on one of the large cymbals with the right hand while adding accents with the left hand on the snare drum. The foot-operated hi-hat, hitting on the second and fourth beats, is conventionally added, although it need not be. Sometimes (often on the first chorus and less often on the last chorus) the hi-hat may be played with the right hand stick, a technique that is excellent for passages, especially introductions or interludes, which have no 4/4 double bass or bass drum.

For a fast tempo the best use of brushes is on the snare. Used in this way, both brushes "stir soup"; that is, they create a sibilant sound which is continuous but must suggest the pulse of the piece. The brushes may also be used on the single cymbal or the hi-hat. When brushes are used on snare or single cymbal, as with sticks on the single cymbal, it is traditional for the hi-hat to be played on two and four, although it would seem even less necessary. In fact, the axiomatic use of hi-hat on the second and fourth beats and the use of 4/4 bass drum is likely to become obsolescent—and rightly so.

There are three types of slow tempos employed in the tradition of the jazz orchestra: A. The jazz "ballad" tempo is very slow. Its pulsation or "beat" is implied more than stated, while the figures are sustained. There is little syncopation. B. The slow, swinging tempo may range from very slow to moderately slow. The beat is stated directly. Great use is made of syncopation. The nature of piece may even be "bluesy." C. The dance or fox trot tempo consists of a very definite statement of the beat, although more for ease of dancing than for artistic purposes.

A.   On the jazz ballad, a great deal of freedom of percussion treatment is possible. Usually the bass drum is used only to outline parts, especially accents, played by other instruments. The hi-hat is not used at all. The feeling of implicit time or pulsation may be obtained through use of brushes on snare or, less advisable, on the single cymbal(s).

Sticks or mallets may be used on the single cymbal(s) or the gong either in connection with orchestral passages (especially for accents and eccentric figures)

or as a foil or counterpoint to orchestral passages. As a foil, the cym-

bal figure may be used preceding, within, or after the orchestral passage.

The cymbal can be attacked and allowed to let ring or a continuous
sound may be created through a roll. The best way to notate a percussion roll is:

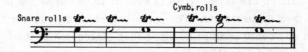

The triangle may also be used in conjunction with orchestral passages. It is likely that these passages will be of an undramatic, lyrical
nature. The triangle is often used to "embroider" very delicate figures.
Here is an example of embroidering <u>within</u> a figure:

B.   On slow, swinging tempos, the drums are treated very much as
they are on faster tempos. Here, though, extensive use can be made of
elaborate fill-in and prefatory figures. Greater freedom is possible because the drums' responsibility to hold the orchestra together is less on
a slow tempo—a fast tempo can fall apart in two beats.

C.   For dance tempos, the most simple drum writing will suffice.
Usually, the bass drum plays a very soft "two" ("two-beat"), consisting
of a quarter note on the first and third beat of each measure. The brushes either stir soup or play on the single cymbal.

In slow music the following should be avoided: the 4/4 bass drum;

any use of the hi-hat besides the slightest "chhi" on the second and fourth beats of the measure; any use of mallets; and, finally, frilly brush figures on the single cymbal(s).

19   THE DOUBLE BASS

The role of the double bass in the jazz orchestra is rhythmic and harmonic: the bass states the pulsation directly or with slight modification; it plays those tones of the chord which help to indicate the harmonic basis. The double bass is almost always used pizzicato (plucked) rather than arco (bowed).

A.   For faster pieces, the bass plays a quarter note line. There are four methods of choosing the tones for the bass line.

1.   Primary use of the roots and fifths of chords:

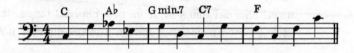

2.   Primary use of root and fifth, with occasional use, as passing tones, of less usual and non-chordal tones to connect the line:

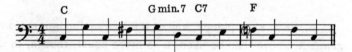

3.   Use of the basic tones of the chord (the first three or four tones), with occasional use of less usual tones to connect the line:

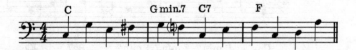

4.   Use of all the possible tones of the chord, in addition to occasional passing tones, neighboring tones, and auxiliary tones—

the non-chordal tones most often occurring on the weaker beats of the bar:

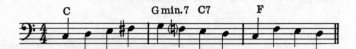

The bass line can consist of either repeated or non-repeated tones. There is a tendency to use repeated tones when the harmonies are of greater duration and a tendency to use non-repeated tones when the harmonic rhythm is faster.

Also, the first two types of bass lines (above) can be either interlocking or non-interlocking. (The third and fourth are always interlocking). "Interlocking" refers to the stepwise motion between chords—especially after a tendency tone (in fact, a line which is basically not interlocking will interlock—a tendency tone at the end of one chord locking into the following tone).

5. For moderately fast pieces or for medium tempos, the "skipping" bass figure is often used. Here (below), the main use is of root and fifth, although the pickup notes (the eighth notes) can be chosen from the other basic chordal tones or from less usual chordal tones or from non-chordal tones. It is best if the pickup notes proceed stepwise into the quarter notes.

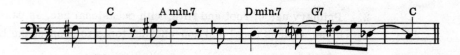

B. For slow pieces, any of the five methods mentioned in paragraph A, above, can be used. It is more usual, though, to write parts like this, with main use of root and fifth:

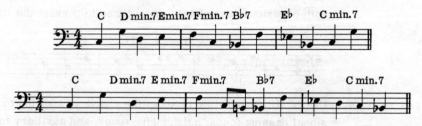

or like this for any type of simple, repeated rhythmic pattern (the basic tones of the chord are usually employed here):

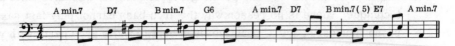

C.   The bass should form a good relationship with the lead (see chap. 27) of the melody. If possible, it should move in contrary or oblique motion to the lead. The octave, thirds, sixths, perfect fifths can be used anywhere. Major seconds, minor sevenths, and augmented fourths can be used but with greater care (they are less dissonant when formed between basic tones of the chord). Other intervals should be treated gingerly.

D.   In addition, however, the bass can, especially on slow pieces, where the rhythmic function is not so important, assume a more direct melodic function.

1.   It can be used for repeated figures which continue unchanging against the upper strata of the composition.

2.   It can outline parts played by other instruments (especially the other bass instruments—bass trombone, baritone saxophone, etc.); this process of outline does not require an exact duplication of the orchestral parts—the bass may play a more traditional role, only joining the other bass instruments on particularly important or significant tones of the passage.

E.   The bowed bass has great facility. Unfortunately, however, the use of pizzicato in jazz has bred a group of bassists who have little arco technique. There is no reason why the arco bass cannot play fast saxophone figures. In actual practice, it is best to write arco parts with very simple technical requirements. The most common uses of arco bass are:

1.   As a pedal point:

2.   With another bass instrument (especially for ensembles):

3.   As an <u>additional</u> bass voice to a section of instruments voiced in open position:

The arco bass is better used when the tempo is slow. It may be used freely when the bass's pulse-stating function is not important.

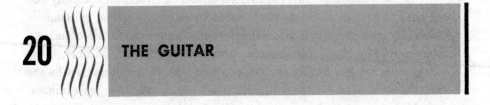

20 THE GUITAR

The guitar can be used with or without amplification. Some guitarists use one guitar for amplified passages and a second for other passages. A sense of the different instrumental qualities most desirable for each use underlies this practice. For most practical purposes, however, it is only necessary to specify that a passage requires amplification or does not.

The use of the 4/4 guitar must be very carefully controlled. It should be employed only on faster tempos to bind the double bass and drums and should be felt rather than heard. The guitarist should not use too sharp or percussive an attack on each quarter beat. He should play softly.

For 4/4, the guitar should be used without amplification. 4/4 guitar parts are written like this:

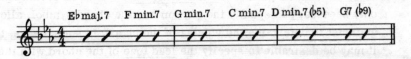

Deviations from absolute adherence to the repeated quarter notes should only occur when the entire rhythm section deviates, which would happen only during the most unusual and pronounced rhythms of the other instruments, most likely in ensemble parts.

The use of the 4/4 guitar should be maintained throughout the entire piece or movement or section. Its irregular use destroys the totality of the 4/4 flow.

"Accommodating" harmonizations of non-chordal tones usually do not need to be indicated; the basic harmony is not disturbed by them. Generally, the chord symbols will correspond with the forms of harmony played by other instruments of the orchestra. For example, if the saxophones are sustaining an open position F69, this will usually be the chord symbol used for the 4/4 guitar part. When the other instruments are playing a sparse harmonic role (for example, a unison line played by trumpets), the guitar part should contain all four-note chords or all five-note chords, depending on the fullness of harmony desired.

It is unwise to allow the guitarist to use additions and alterations of his own choice. It is not good to write the most basic form of the chord, expecting him to make proper use of additions and alterations.

The guitar may also be used for chordal feeding, a function very similar to the pianist's in small jazz groups: the guitarist "lays down" the harmonic framework, employing simple rhythmic figures. This type of guitar part may be written exactly, although it is usually safe to allow the guitarist to use his own discretion. "Chordal ad lib" is a good term to indicate that the guitarist is to improvise a background of this sort.

The parts for improvised chordal feeding are written exactly like those for the 4/4 guitar. When writing out the chordal feeding part, it is only necessary to specify the rhythm and the chord symbol, allowing the guitarist to determine the voicing of the chord. In some cases, though, it may be desirable to specify the lead tone of the chord with the alphabetical symbol and the rhythm. The guitarist then uses a voicing which will match the symbol and the lead tone.

Chordal feeding of this sort is more useful for faster tempos.

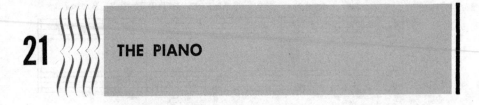

21 THE PIANO

The complete range of the piano is:

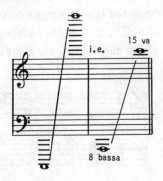

The use of the piano in the jazz orchestra has been incomplete and indiscriminate. While the piano is a magnificent and large instrument, it has rarely been treated as such. Instead, it has been used as a general filler with little concern for its possibilities.

The piano should be used only when needed. Except for actual solo passages, the pianist should have less and less of an improvisatory role. Specific figures can and should be written for the piano.

Improvised chordal feeding can be used on either fast or slow pieces though it is not necessary for the piano to feed throughout a piece. It is best that feeding take place when the figures of the wind instruments are very simple or when the rhythm section is playing by itself or behind a soloist.

The part for improvised chordal feeding can be written in two ways: (a) just as the 4/4 guitar part, with the alphabetical symbols and the ver- gules; and (b) with two staffs, the upper just as the 4/4 guitar part, and the lower staff containing an exact duplication of the double bass part (written an octave lower than the double bass part) which serves to guide voicings and harmonies of the pianist. This double bass part is not meant to be played.

Written chordal parts of any kind present almost no limitation for the piano. It is suggested that the rules of voicing be heeded even though the piano's lack of ability to sustain reduces their importance somewhat. Six-tone open position chords are very easily applied to this instrument.

A main consideration in writing for the piano is that the piano "absorbs" sounds very well—it minimizes dissonant structures. Consequently, a chord which would be terrifying in its impact if voiced for brass will be relatively mild when played on the piano. This fact can be turned around: much clear and clean wind instrument writing sounds weak when played on the piano. The piano is inadequate as the sole criterion of orchestral writing. It does not give a representation of the orchestra.

22   A PRELIMINARY VIEW OF THE ENSEMBLE

The craft of ensemble writing is dearly acquired. It is one of the most difficult tasks of orchestration. There are four primary ensemble methods. At first, it is best to maintain strict separation of the four methods, although later two or even three of these methods may be combined in the same passage. Each ensemble method should be learned thoroughly in its elementary form.

As used in jazz composing, "ensemble" means that all the wind instruments are playing at the same time and that they are playing the same figures—the same rhythms. The ensemble, then, is an immense expansion of a melody line.

The orchestral information in this text concerns the traditional jazz orchestra which consists of trumpets, trombones, saxophones, and a rhythm section (piano, bass, drums, and sometimes guitar). Ensemble writing for this type of orchestra is mainly a problem of combining the brass section with the saxophones. The rhythm section will either continue to supply the pulse, give additional support to the wind instruments, or be silent during ensembles.

The most important consideration is that the brass must always be independent of the saxophones. The saxophones in an ideal ensemble are to be felt and not heard. They are the backbone of the ensemble but the less they are noticed—as reed instruments—the better. The ideal ensemble is characterized by a veiled brass sound—brass softened by saxophones.

23 THE BASIC ENSEMBLE METHOD

The basic ensemble method is applicable to melodies of limited range and heavy, majestic character. A melody to be so treated should not extend more than a perfect fifth, especially when the group for which it is being written is fairly large (eight brass and five saxophones, for example).

A.   First, the brass must be voiced in close position, carefully following all the rules and suggestions contained in the previous chapters. The lowest brass part should be more often than is otherwise usual dropped to the root or the fifth of the chord.

B.   After the brass have been voiced, the saxophones should be added. The saxophones should play fairly simple open position voicings. The lead alto should never be above the lead trumpet and should preferably be at least a fourth below. If the lowest brass part is in the low baritone saxophone range, the baritone saxophone should double it. Avoid parallel motion leading into octaves between brass and saxophones.

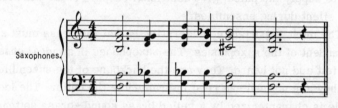

C.   The saxophone voicings may contain tones not in the brass voicings. It is permissible that the brass play a C6 while the saxophones are playing a C69. The saxophones should not, though, play contradictory tones. That is, the saxophones should not play a lowered ninth while the brass play an unaltered ninth. The <u>additional</u> tones need not correspond, but the <u>altered</u> tones must correspond.

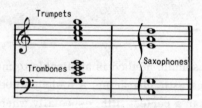

D.   The saxophones need not strictly follow the contour of the brass. When the brass move to another position of the same chord, it is not necessary for the saxophones to change positions unless the second chord is accented or there is a space between the two chords. The saxophones will not always play all the figures of the brass—sometimes they will simply sustain chords beneath them. The saxophones must

sound only when the brass sound—neither more nor less. This is strict
ensemble writing.

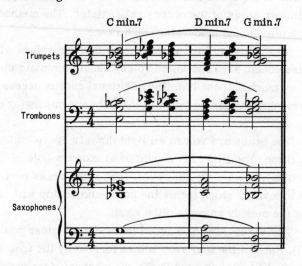

THE FOUR-TONE ENSEMBLE METHOD

The basic ensemble method was outlined in the previous chapter. As
noted, it is most suitable for melodies of limited range and of simple
rhythmic nature.

Different techniques are required for different circumstances. A
melody consisting of many eighth or sixteenth notes, with few if any sustained notes, and of a distinctly melodic nature, made up of much stepwise motion—such a melody must be treated entirely differently than the
slow-moving and harmonic melody for which the first ensemble method
is suited.

Large chords and thick voicing are not appropriate to a fast-moving
melody and would create difficult lines for all the lower parts, especially if the melody utilizes extensive range, which is likely. A melody of
this type needs a clear, slender harmonization and a graceful approximation of the lead line by the harmony parts.

A.   Although the range of four-tone ensemble is likely to be greater than that of the basic ensemble, it should not extend up into the higher and thinner areas of the orchestral register. The method is best suited for the middle and moderately high range.

B.   All the tones of the melody must be harmonized with four-tone chords (see chap. 15). The lower voices should simulate the motion of the lead as much as possible. The additional chords necessary for four-tone harmonization can be found in the lists accompanying chapters 14 and 15.

C.   The brass are voiced straight down in "pure" thickened line close position. The fifth part should be an exact double of the second part, an octave lower, etc. However, the lowest brass part may be dropped to a voice which forms the best relationship with the lead part. Doubling the melody voice is often good.

D.   The saxophones are added in "widened" close position (see chap. 17). Each of the four real voices formed by the four-tone harmonization must be represented in the saxophones; if there are five saxophones, one of the real voices will be duplicated in another octave.

The spatial relationship between saxophones and brass in this ensemble method will be similar to that in the basic ensemble method. The lead saxophone should be assigned to a voice beneath the lead trumpet. The other saxophones should be assigned the remaining voices, alternate and adjacent. The baritone saxophone should be kept in its lowest octave. If the lowest brass part lies here, the two instruments can be doubled. When the lowest brass part is above or below this octave, the baritone saxophone should be assigned a voice which is at least two voices above the lowest brass part (if it is too low) or two voices beneath the lowest brass part (if it is too high).

Eight brass (four trumpets and four trombones) and five saxophones (two alto saxophones, two tenor saxophones, and baritone saxophone) are employed in the following example. Here it would be best to double the first alto with the third trumpet, the second alto with the first trombone, the first tenor with the second trombone, the second tenor with the fourth trombone, and the baritone an octave lower than the second trombone.

The range of the passage in question will always affect the distribution of the saxophones. It must be remembered that each of the four different voices must be represented in the saxophones.

25 THE PERCUSSIVE ENSEMBLE METHOD

The percussive ensemble method is designed for extremely rhythmic melodies. Harmonic rather than melodic, it is not designed for flowing melodies. It is a wall of sound and should be applied to melodies of limited range, preferably not more than a third.

The percussive ensemble method requires large groups of instruments to create bulk and power.

A.   The lead or melody tones which permit the fullest harmonization are best. These include the extensions, such as ninths, elevenths, etc., in addition to fifths (which can be treated as twelfths), thirds (which can be treated as tenths), etc. The melody line formed by these tones should not embrace more than a perfect fifth, at the most. Small range is the special characteristic of this method.

B.   Only one lead tone should be used for each chord. If the chordal area extends for more than a measure, two tones from the chord may be used to form the melody if: (a) they are separated by at least a quarter-note rest; (b) they are more than a major second apart.

C.   The top brass parts should be voiced as closely as possible (within the restrictions of close position voicing). When eight or more brass are used, the lower voices should be spread, almost forming open positions.

If six or more brass are used, the very top trumpet and trombone registers may be utilized for this ensemble.

D.   The saxophones should be added, as in the basic ensemble
method, in open position voicings. Here, though, the positions will be
very limited. Frequent use should be made of root-fifth or fifth-root
in the two lowest saxophone parts. The two or three lowest saxophone
parts should correspond exactly with the two or three lowest brass
parts when these brass parts extend fairly low.

Sometimes the bass trombone will be beneath the baritone saxophone
range and the baritone saxophone will have to double the next-to-lowest
trombone part.

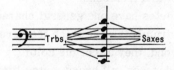

In complete form, the percussive ensemble will look like this:

26   BRASS MUTES

Here and throughout this book, reference to brass instruments includes only the trumpet and trombone.

All brass mutes have one general characteristic: they change the sound of the instruments with which they are used. First, they lessen the volume; second, they affect the color.

In varying degrees, all brass mutes limit the instrument. Extremes of register are cut off; technically difficult passages are more difficult; quick-moving passages sometimes do not get out of the instruments—the mute has "bottled" the sound; good intonation is harder to achieve; the act of articulating the sound—the first tonguing—is more difficult.

There are two main types of brass mutes:

1.   Mutes which fit into the bell of the instrument: cup, straight, and harmon. These mutes drastically alter and greatly soften the sound of the instrument.

2.   Mutes which fit over or around the bell of the instrument:

(a) the tight plunger and felt hat, which touch the instrument; (b) the loose plunger and metal derby (hat), which are held away from the instrument. The loose plunger, felt hat, and derby alter the sound of the instruments much less than any of the other mutes. These three mutes serve more to "cover" the sound.

The original version of the plunger is the plumbing plunger, turned inside out and pierced through the center with a small hole. A manufactured version is now generally available.

The plunger may be used in two ways: (a) pressed firmly against the bell of the horn, or (b) tilted away, with one edge touching the bottom of the bell. The first is notated as "tight" plunger, the second as "loose" plunger.

For solos and quasi-solos, the plumbing plunger is preferable. For tight plunger work, it is absolutely necessary, since the manufactured plunger seriously disturbs the intonation and the tone-attack. On the other hand, the manufactured plunger is likely to get superior results when used for a choir of brass in loose plunger; it produces a more uniform sound. The tight plunger deadens the sound of the instrument. Its most effective use is for powerful passages, which barely seep through the muting.

The most conventional use of the tight plunger is in alternation with punctuations or short figures which are played open. This is the only mute which can be so used with great contrast. The alternation of the hat and "open" is not as marked a contrast.

The loose plunger can be very effective. It closes the sound a little more than the hat. It is excellent for middle range passages, preferably

soft and/or simple. It allows a little more maneuverability than the hat.
The plunger cannot be used for bass trombone beneath F.

The harmon mute is excellent for the trumpet, but no satisfactory
form has been made for the trombone. Its use for the low register (the
lowest octave of the trumpet) is not recommended. Intonation in this area
with this mute is almost impossible to control. In the hands of a fairly
good player, the harmon mute can be very well used in the upper register. The very highest tones are precluded, of course.

There are two detachable parts of the harmon mute. First is the
rod which penetrates the center of the mute. Attached to this is a small
cone. The parts can be varied in these ways: the mute can be played
without them; the rod alone can be used; the rod (with or without the
cone) can be extended in varying degrees from the center of the mute.
These fine distinctions between the forms of the harmon mute should be
observed and carefully indicated in the score.

The sound of the harmon mute is light, dry, and metallic. It is more
like the rustle of silver foil than the smack of a hammer on an anvil. The
harmon mute slows down the speaking of the instrument considerably.
For this reason, accented and choppy figures should be written with care.
Enough space should be included between the notes of the figure so that
they can take shape.

The harmon mute is excellent for sustained and legato passages.
When harmonized, these passages should be high enough so that the lowest voices can sound out.

More than any other mute, the harmon mute separates the sound of a brass instrument from other instruments. For this reason, it may be used to minimize or clearly define harmonic and melodic "clashes."

To get an over-all harmon mute sound from the brass section, the trombones should use straight mutes. If no straight mutes are available, the trombones may use cup mutes. In fact, the cup may also be used in the trombones when the trumpets are playing with straights.

The cup mute is the basic brass mute. It is equally efficient for trumpet or trombone. It disturbs the proper playing of the instrument less than any mute of its type (see 1, above). There are three variable factors connected with the use of the cup mute: (a) the use of a felt lining on the inside of the "cup," (b) the use of rubber edging on the rim of the "cup," and (c) the tightness or closeness of fit, which can be increased by shaving down the corks on the side of the mute. The use of rubber edging with the felt (and/or a handkerchief), plus a very tight fitting, will obtain maximum deadness and softness of sound.

The cup mute is excellent for any combination of brass instruments. It can be used for sustained or figured passages and all but the very loudest dynamics are possible. The cup mute produces an exquisite pianissimo. The lower range of the instrument is limited more than the higher by this mute.

The metal derby or hat is a muting device rather than a mute. It affects the sound of the instrument the least, although it can cause distortion when used with too great volume or in the high register. Since it slows down the "speaking" of the instruments, it is best used for sustained sound. The derby is especially effective for simple, soft passages. For best results, the bell of the horn must be centered and kept a respectful three inches from the rim of the hat.

One of the main advantages of the derby is that it makes more uniform the combined sound of trumpets and trombones by cutting down the edge or brilliance of the trumpets. Its hollow and remote sound is one of the most useful tools of the jazz writer.

Especially for the trombones, it is best to use the derby with a supporting stand in order to free both of the player's hands for his instrument. And this makes possible very quick changes, from hat to open and from open to hat.

To create gradations of the muted effect ("doo-wa," "wa-doo," etc.), the player must hold the derby in his left hand. It is difficult to play either the trumpet or the trombone without the pressure of both hands. When the derby is required to be held in the left hand, then, the brass should not be written in the upper register. An additional problem with the trombone is that only those tones obtainable in the first, second, third, and fourth positions can be used, since the player cannot maintain

the balance of the instrument in the remaining three positions when his
left hand is at the bell.

The straight mute is similar to the cup mute in these respects:
(a) it alters the tone of the instrument greatly; (b) it limits the higher
register less than the low register; and (c) it allows more freedom of
execution than other mutes. It is not quite as flexible as the cup mute
and its sustained quality is not as good. Its use for trombone is particularly limited, requiring a good player and a good mute. (Often, individual mutes within a good brand line are not themselves good, making this
situation more complicated.)

For percussive passages the straight mute is excellent as its pene-
tration and directness are exceeded by no other mute. It is not good for
legato, melodic phrases.

27   THE BACKGROUND

Some points about writing backgrounds are outlined below. The real
problem is getting a proper "balance" between the melody and its accompaniment.

Balance has nothing to do with volume. Rather, it is the proper
combination of orchestral colors, the proper combination of characteristics of the foreground melody and background melody. The background
must be defined and separated from the foreground; background and foreground must complement each other.

The background is usually sustained or silent when the melody is active rhythmically.

When the melody is sustained or silent, the background is usually more active rhythmically.

The background should usually enter before the melody which it is to accompany. The melody then "steps" on the carpet established by the background. The two should never begin at exactly the same time.

There is no problem of conflict between a single-tone line, whether it be the melody or the background, and any of the lower parts of a chordal unit. There is a conflict, however, between the top part of a chordal unit and a single-tone line, as there is between two single-tone lines.

For clarity it will be better to use one term for both the single-tone line and for the line formed by the top tones of a chordal unit; both will be called the "lead."

The lead of the background and the lead of the melody should not form certain intervals, except for the shortest moment. These intervals are of two classes. The first consists of the minor second, major seventh, and minor ninth. They should be avoided because they confuse the relationship between the lines. They are too harsh. The second class of undesirable intervals consists of the prime, the octave, and the double octave. These intervals are not good for an opposite and yet identical reason: they are so closely related to each other that they "run together" and consequently obscure the separation between the two lines.

Note Well: The discussion of melodic relationship between foreground and background is necessarily only an introductory suggestion to the enormous topic of counterpoint. It is beyond the scope of this book for the author to do more in this area than relieve the student of one or two of the most obvious and painful problems.

28 THE PLANNING OF ORCHESTRATION

A. When the foreground melody is a single-tone line (a solo or a group of instruments in unison or octaves), the background can be either single-tone or chordal.

B. When the foreground is chordal, the background should not be chordal (unless the foreground is made up of fragments and the background enters only between the fragments).

C. The ensemble should be employed sparingly. This is especially true of the large and loud ensemble.

D. Generally, an orchestral unit should not be assigned the foreground for one passage and the background for the following passage. Not as bad, though not advisable, is the reverse procedure: an orchestral unit used as the background for one passage and as foreground for the following passage. Alternation is most undesirable when the orchestral unit is treated the same way both times (e.g., close position saxophones playing the melody for one phrase and then, voiced the same way, playing background for the following passage).

E. Technically, it is always better to err on the side of simplicity than on the side of complexity. Music which is beneath the technical level of the musicians will be played well. Music that is the slightest bit too hard may not be played at all.

F. The comfortable areas of the instruments should be used for graceful and lyrical passages. The areas of the instrument that involve strain and tension should not be utilized except for passages that are dramatic and powerful.

G. Generally, the instrument(s) assigned the melody and the instrument(s) assigned the background should not be from the same section. If they are, however, care should be taken that their similarity is diminished, through voicing, or use of mutes, etc.

H. Similar combinations of instruments (see following chapter) should not be used for adjoining passages.

I. The orchestration should coincide with the music. In beginning terms, this rule means that an eight-bar melody will not begin with unison trombones and conclude with close position saxophones. Change of orchestration should accompany change of musical material.

It is perhaps more important to understand the following qualifications to this statement than the statement itself:

1. It is possible, through use of many and varied combinations of instruments and through the avoidance of the usual orchestral units (trumpets or trombones or saxophones), to treat the entire jazz orchestra as one single body. This single body may have many varieties of color and nuances of sound but it will be a unit rather than a combination of three or four orchestral choirs. If the jazz orchestra is so treated (and the beginning student is not advised to follow such a course), a given melodic line can be passed frequently from one instrument or group of instruments to another without destroying the union of form and orchestration.

2. If the melody itself is in reality two melodies (a melody which,

for example, dips down to answer itself), its treatment may be sensibly divided.

3.   If a certain part of the melody needs to be stressed, an instrument may be added to reinforce this part.

4.   When the background is more an accompaniment than an independent melody, it is possible to make orchestral changes fairly easily.

J.   Sometimes, the key of part of the piece or even of the entire piece will be changed so that the orchestration which best brings out the music can be accommodated.

29   COMBINATIONS OF INSTRUMENTS

Below are sixty-five possible combinations of instruments. The list is not complete. These combinations can be used out of necessity (because no others are available) or to alter the general texture of a larger group of instruments from which they were drawn.

The more usual combinations are intermixed with those which are less usual. As a general rule, the rarer combinations of instruments resist prolonged use and do not have as much flexibility as those which are well known and thoroughly investigated.

The listings are to be read from left to right and represent the position of the instruments from high to low.

   1.   ALTO ALTO TENOR TENOR

   2.   ALTO TENOR TENOR TENOR

Both of these combinations are best treated with the thickened line. Number 1 is fluffier than 2 because of the additional alto.

   3.   ALTO ALTO TENOR BARITONE

   4.   ALTO TENOR TENOR BARITONE

   5.   TENOR TENOR TENOR BARITONE

   6.   TENOR ALTO TENOR BARITONE

These combinations are best treated with the thickened line. Open position is good for 3 and 4 and may be used for 5. When treated with the thickened line, 5 is the "Four Brothers" sound. Number 6 is merely an imitation of 5 and should not be used unless required.

    7. ALTO ALTO TENOR TENOR BARITONE

    8. ALTO TENOR TENOR TENOR BARITONE

The above two combinations are good for regular close position voicing and open position voicing. When the thickened line is applied, the baritone should double either the lead alto an octave lower or the second voice an octave lower. The widened thickened line is particularly good for either of these combinations since each has an extensive aggregate range.

    9. ALTO TENOR TROMBONE TENOR

   10. ALTO TENOR TROMBONE BARITONE

These combinations are called the "gazelle" sound. For both the very best use is with the thickened line. Open position voicing is suggested only for 10. Valve trombone is better than slide trombone with either combination.

   11. TROMBONE TENOR TROMBONE TENOR

   12. TROMBONE TENOR TROMBONE BARITONE

The best use of these two combinations employs the thickened line. Open position is suggested only for 12. Either valve or slide trombones can be used. Bass trombone is not advisable.

   13. TRUMPET ALTO TROMBONE TENOR

   14. TRUMPET TENOR TROMBONE TENOR

   15. TRUMPET ALTO TROMBONE BARITONE

   16. TRUMPET TENOR TROMBONE BARITONE

All four of these combinations may be treated with close position and thickened line. Only 15 and 16 are good for open position or widened line. The trumpet should be kept beneath top line F of the treble clef. The lower the trumpet is, the better (excluding written low c♯1, g, f♯).

   17. TENOR TROMBONE

   18. TROMBONE TENOR

Either of the above is an excellent unison or duet combination. Both are especially good when the trombone is not taken too high and the tenor is not taken too low. Valve trombone is best. Bass trombone is not suggested.

   19. TROMBONE TROMBONE TROMBONE TROMBONE

   20. TROMBONE TROMBONE TROMBONE BASS TROMBONE

Either of these combinations may be voiced in close position, including the thickened line and the widened line (if range permits). Open position voicing may be used for either and is especially good for 20.

21. TROMBONE TROMBONE TROMBONE TROMBONE TROM-
    BONE

22. TROMBONE TROMBONE TROMBONE TROMBONE BASS
    TROMBONE

The preceding paragraph also applies to these combinations. Open
position voicing for 21 should not encompass too large a range.

23. TRUMPET TRUMPET TRUMPET TRUMPET

24. TRUMPET TRUMPET TRUMPET TROMBONE

Close position voicing, including the thickened line, is very good
for either of these combinations.

25. TRUMPET TRUMPET TROMBONE TROMBONE

26. TRUMPET TRUMPET TROMBONE TROMBONE TROMBONE

27. TRUMPET TRUMPET TROMBONE TROMBONE BASS TROM-
    BONE

These three combinations may be treated with close position voicing or open position voicing. The thickened line or widened line may also
be used.

28. TRUMPET TROMBONE TROMBONE TROMBONE

29. TRUMPET TROMBONE TROMBONE BASS TROMBONE

These may be treated with close position, including the thickened
line and the widened line. The latter is very appropriate (especially for
29) because of the large range these combined instruments have. Open
position voicing is very good for either combination.

30. TRUMPET TRUMPET TRUMPET TROMBONE TROMBONE

31. TRUMPET TRUMPET TRUMPET TROMBONE BASS TROM-
    BONE

Close position may be used for either of these combinations. The
thickened line or the widened line may be used if called for. Although
open position voicing is sometimes used for three trumpets with only
two trombones, it is not suggested.

32. 3 TRUMPETS 3 TROMBONES

33. 3 TRUMPETS 2 TROMBONES BASS TROMBONE

Either of these combinations may be voiced in close position or
open position. The thickened line or widened line may be used if called
for.

34. 3 TRUMPETS 4 TROMBONES

35. 3 TRUMPETS 3 TROMBONES BASS TROMBONE

36. 4 TRUMPETS   4 TROMBONES
37. 4 TRUMPETS   3 TROMBONES   BASS TROMBONE

Any of the above combinations may be voiced in close position, including the thickened line or the widened line (if possible). Open position voicing may be used for these combinations, probably very close at the top and open at the bottom because of the larger number of instruments. (The sound of trumpets becomes thin when they are spread apart.)

38. 5 TRUMPETS   3 TROMBONES
39. 5 TRUMPETS   2 TROMBONES   BASS TROMBONE
40. 5 TRUMPETS   4 TROMBONES
41. 5 TRUMPETS   3 TROMBONES   BASS TROMBONE
42. 5 TRUMPETS   5 TROMBONES
43. 5 TRUMPETS   4 TROMBONES   BASS TROMBONE
44. 6 TRUMPETS   5 TROMBONES
45. 6 TRUMPETS   4 TROMBONES   BASS TROMBONE

These eight combinations may be voiced in close position, including the thickened line. The widened line is seldom possible here because of the number of instruments.

46. ALTO   3 TROMBONES
47. ALTO   2 TROMBONES   BASS TROMBONE
48. ALTO   4 TROMBONES
49. ALTO   3 TROMBONES   BASS TROMBONE

These four combinations are best used in open position. Five-tone chords are better for 48 and 49 because the doubled tone in four-tone chords will often impair the complete blending of the alto saxophone and the trombones.

50. TRUMPET ALTO TENOR TENOR BARITONE
51. TRUMPET ALTO ALTO TENOR BARITONE
52. TRUMPET TENOR TENOR TENOR BARITONE

The above combinations may be used in all the various forms of close position (thickened line is best). With thickened line or widened line, it is best if one of the saxophones doubles the trumpet an octave below; this will avoid two saxophones unduly reinforcing one voice and disturbing the blend. These combinations are fine for open position voicings, especially when the trumpet uses loose plunger.

53. TRUMPET ALTO TROMBONE TENOR TROMBONE
54. TRUMPET ALTO TROMBONE TENOR BASS TROMBONE

55. TRUMPET TENOR TROMBONE TENOR TROMBONE

56. TRUMPET TENOR TROMBONE TENOR BASS TROMBONE

These four combinations are best used for open position voicing, with the brass instruments in hat or with loose plunger. If used for close position voicing (especially with thickened or widened line), it is very important that no brass part doubles another brass voice and that no saxophone part doubles another saxophone voice. For any kind of close voicing, the brass may use straight mutes or cup mutes with good effect.

57. ALTO TROMBONE TENOR TROMBONE BARITONE

58. ALTO TROMBONE TENOR BASS TROMBONE BARITONE

Combinations 57 and 58 are best for open position voicing. For all uses, the two trombones should be in hats or with loose plunger. When used for close writing, care must be taken that the trombone parts do not double each other and that the saxophone parts do not double each other.

59. ALTO TRUMPET

60. TRUMPET ALTO

61. TRUMPET TENOR

62. ALTO TROMBONE

63. TROMBONE ALTO

The problem with all these combinations is range. The trumpet must not go too high or too low. The alto must not scrape the bottom. The trombone must not go too high. These combinations may be used for unisons or for any duet combinations (thirds, sixths, especially). Sixths are particularly good for 61 and 62.

64. 4 TRUMPETS BARITONE

65. 5 TRUMPETS BARITONE

For both of these combinations the trumpets should be in close position. It is best if they are muted. Harmons or loose plungers are especially good. The baritone may be placed an octave or so beneath the lowest trumpet. This part may be one of the trumpet voices or a separate bass voice. The baritone part should be simultaneous with the trumpet parts and should be rhythmically identical. This sound is best for sustained passages.

30   IDENTITIES

The same tone played at the same time by two or more instruments is a unison. The unison is an identity—the separate tones form one reinforced tone. The octave and the double octave form a "mirroring" of one tone. They are also identities. In orchestral terms, though, a unison is not the same as an octave or double octave.

The tones of a unison especially, and to a lesser degree those of octaves and double octaves, tend to clasp one another. They reinforce one another. Much less individuality of phrasing is possible on a unison than on a voiced passage.

The volume of a unison is greater than that produced by the same instruments playing a chord. Two trombones playing middle C will automatically be louder than two trombones playing middle C and the E above it, even though each of the players makes no change in volume level. Octaves and double octaves are also louder. It is best, then, to notate unisons at a lower dynamic level than chordal passages, unless this greater volume is desired.

Identities make discrepancies of intonation more obvious. They also make differences of performance more obvious. For these reasons identities should be used with care for passages which are in extremes of range or which involve difficult notes for the instrument.

Use of identities in writing is good. It encourages melodic thinking. Writing which contains very few identities is usually too harmonic in its basis.

The instrument which is in its most natural range will usually dominate an identity, having greater ease and control of tone production. However, an extremely high or extremely low part (especially when heavy and loud) will dominate any unison or octave combination.

Within a group of the same instruments, unisons are usually better than octaves and almost always better than double octaves. Most wind instruments do not have a large enough range to be stretched across an octave or more. They cannot balance. When passages are very high or very low, however, it is better to use octaves than to keep all the instruments in an extreme range.

It must be kept in mind that there are differences of <u>sound</u> between the unison and the octave and the double octave. Despite the directions below, then, sometimes it will be desirable to use one in preference to the other. For example, the octave has an intensity which is greater than the unison. When this intensity is desired, a lower octave may be added. Also, the true unison has a purity which any form of the octave lacks. When this purity is necessary, the lower octave must not be used.

1.   A change of range between two adjacent phrases can be easily accommodated by changing the distribution for each phrase. For example, a middle register phrase for trumpets would be assigned a true unison; if it is followed by a high register phrase, the trumpets (four, say) can be split into octaves.

2.   A change of range <u>within</u> the phrase can be handled in two ways: (a) by choosing a distribution which will suit the different registers, even though imperfect for a smaller part of the phrase, or (b) by changing the distribution within the phrase—here, it is best to change at a point which involves the smallest skip for the instruments. For example, a trumpet phrase begins with a few tones in the middle register; these tones are in unison; then the phrase leaps up into the upper register, requiring part of the section to play a lower octave—when the lower trumpets change to the lower octave, they should do so by the minimum skip possible.

A. TRUMPETS

1. On high parts, as many as possible (not too far exceeding half) of the trumpets should be placed in the upper octave. The remainder should be an octave below.

2. On middle range parts, it is best if all the trumpets are in unison.

3. For low parts, it is best if all the trumpets are in unison. If this is not possible, more than half should be in the lowest octave and the remainder an octave above.

B. TROMBONES

1. On high parts, as many as possible (not exceeding half) of the trombones should be placed in the upper octave. The remainder should be an octave below.

2. On middle range parts, it is best if all the trombones are in unison. However, the bass trombone may double middle register parts an octave below, especially if there are three or more tenor trombones in the upper octave.

3.   Low figures are best in unison. Since the trombone speaks so
     well in its low register, low unisons present no problem. If uni-
     son is not possible, the low octave can dominate if played by on-
     ly one trombone (especially a bass trombone) if the passage is
     a heavy and powerful one.

C.   BRASS

1.   For high parts, the brass should usually be divided into double
     octaves. As many trumpets as possible should play the highest
     octave. The remainder of the trumpets and as many of the trom-
     bones as possible (not exceeding half) should play the octave be-
     low. The remainder of the trombones should play the octave be-
     low.

2.   For middle range parts, it is usually best if all the trumpets
     play the upper octave and all the trombones play the lower oc-
     tave. It is possible to have a unison between trumpets and trom-
     bones. The trumpets will play the figure in their middle range
     and the trombones will play the figure in their upper range,
     forming a real unison. This distribution can only be used with-
     in the octave beginning slightly below middle C. It is conse-
     quently very limited. Trombones will dominate the upper tones

or all the tones if the figure is powerful.

3. For low parts, it is best if all the trumpets play the figure in the upper octave and all the trombones double the figure an oc-tave lower.

D. SAXOPHONES

Altos alone should be in unison. Tenors alone should be in unison. Alto and tenor in unison get a tenor sound. Alto and tenor in octaves get an alto sound. Tenor and baritone in unison get a tenor sound. Tenor and baritone in octaves get baritone sound, especially if the figure is heavy and low for the baritone. Alto and baritone in unison get a tenor sound.

Alto an octave above tenor and baritone in unison get an alto sound if high and get a tenor sound otherwise. Alto and tenor in unison and an octave above baritone get a baritone sound if the figure is heavy and low for the baritone. Otherwise, this distribution has a tenor quality.

Double octaves are difficult to use and should be employed only to facilitate an otherwise left-handed passage. Usually the alto and baritone sounds will dominate.

E.   SAXOPHONES AND TROMBONES

1.   For high parts, this combination is best divided into octaves. The altos and as many trombones as possible (not exceeding half) play the upper octave. The other saxophones and remaining trombones play the lower octave.

2.   For middle range parts, a true unison is possible, though octaves are often used here. The altos and tenors play the upper octave with half or more of the trombones (sometimes leaving only one if this remaining one is a bass trombone). The baritone and remaining trombone(s) play an octave below.

3.   For low parts, the altos are often omitted, leaving a true unison. If the figure is heavy, however, and the low octave will dominate, it is possible to use the altos and tenors and a part of the trombone section in the upper octave. The remainder of

the instruments play the lower octave. The success of this division is made more likely by the presence of bass trombone. Keep in mind that the lower octave will sound as the melody octave; the upper octave will merely help the lower octave—it will often hardly be heard.

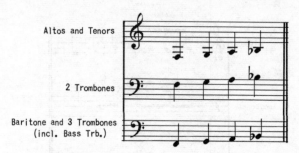

F.   ENSEMBLE (TRUMPETS, TROMBONES, SAXOPHONES)

Identities for the combined wind instruments can be very effective. They are simple and direct and the lack of harmony makes them stand out. Because of the dramatic quality of identity, the character of the music for which it is used must be carefully thought-out. A trite idea is laid bare by any unison, especially an ensemble unison. The absence of the chord places complete responsibility on the excellence of the melodic line.

The ensemble unison is sometimes the only way of treating certain passages. Because there are no harmony parts, the range of an ensemble unison can be great (easily an octave and a fourth). Since a prime melody is almost easier to play than a harmony part, a difficult passage can be more easily negotiated in this form. Some passages contain tones which cannot be set to chords without unnatural results; the unison eliminates the need for the chords. Unisons are particularly useful for passages with much skipping in the melodic line. In fact, the unison is sometimes the only way in which an angularity of line can be accommodated.

1.   For high parts, double octaves are best. As many of the trumpets as possible (not too far exceeding half) should play the highest octave. The remainder of the trumpets, the altos, and as many of the trombones as possible (not too far exceeding half) should play the middle octave. The remainder of the trombones and the baritone play the lowest octave. The tenors will sometimes play the middle octave and sometimes the lower. It

is often wise to divide them between the two lower octaves. This division must be decided on the basis of range and rela- tive strength of each octave.

2. For middle range parts, it is best to put all the instruments in the most <u>comfortable</u> range, in the register that gives the ensemble the most flexibility.

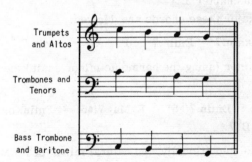

3. A true unison is only possible on the few tones above and below middle C. If the special quality of the octave is desired, or if the passage extends beyond the limited range of the true unison, octaves may be used. The trumpets and altos play the upper oc- tave; the trombones and baritone play the lower octave; the ten-

ors are fitted to their range (their lowest fourth is best avoided unless the passage is loud). Sometimes the bass trombone and baritone play yet another octave below, casting a darker color over the passage; this disposition is usually reserved for majestic and sustained phrases.

31 CHORDS DERIVED FROM SCALES

The material in this chapter is an extension and an expansion of diatonic harmony. These are the chords which may be derived from the basic scales—major and minor. This material should be viewed separately from the other harmonic material.

A.   THE DIATONIC CHORDS.   A chord may be built in thirds on each step of the scale. It is necessary to go up to the seventh when the seventh defines the quality of the chord. (The difference between a major triad and a dominant seventh is in the seventh.) Further additions to the chord may or may not be diatonic. This will conform to the material contained in chapter 3.

In C major these chords are derived:

C   Dmin.7   Emin.7   F   G7   Amin.7   Bmin.7($\flat$5)

In C minor (using the harmonic minor scale) these chords are derived:

Cmin.   Dmin.7($\flat$5)   E$\flat$Maj.7($\sharp$5)   Fmin. or Fmin.7   G7
A$\flat$ B^{o}7

In minor, additionally, the natural minor scale and the melodic minor scale (ascending) are often used. This is almost a necessity for the chord built on III, which is almost never used in the form shown immediately above. These are the new chords, then:

Cmin.7   Dmin.7   E$\flat$ Gmin.7   Amin.7($\flat$5)   B$\flat$

B.   THE SECONDARY DOMINANT SEVENTH CHORDS.   A dominant seventh type chord may be built a perfect fifth above each scale step (in both major and minor) and will have the same relationship to this scale step that <u>the</u> dominant seventh chord (the chord built on the fifth tone of the scale—called the V7) has to the tonic (first tone of the scale).

The secondary dominant seventh chords are notated in reference to their related tone. The secondary dominant seventh of II (D in the C major scale) would be called a V7 of II, usually abbreviated as V7/II. V7/III, then, would mean a dominant seventh type chord built a perfect fifth above the third step of the scale; in the key of C major V7/III would be B7—but in C minor it would be B♭7.

The secondary dominant seventh chords in C major are:

A7   B7   C7   D7   E7   F♯7

The secondary dominant seventh chords in C minor are:

A7   B♭7   C7   D7   E♭7   F♯7

Using the other two minor scales, these additional secondary dominant seventh chords may be derived:

E7   F7

C. THE CHROMATIC DOMINANT SEVENTH CHORDS. A dominant seventh type chord may be built a minor second above each scale step (in both major and minor). The chromatic dominant seventh chords are notated in reference to their related tone. The chromatic dominant seventh of V (G in the C major scale) would be called a chromatic seventh of V. This is more usually abbreviated as Ch7/V. Ch7/II, then, would mean a dominant seventh type chord built a minor second above the second step of the scale; in the key of F major this would be an A♭7—in C minor, this would be an E♭7.

The chromatic dominant seventh chords in C major are:

D♭7   E♭7   F7   G♭7   A♭7   B♭7   C7

The chromatic dominant seventh chords in C minor are:

D♭7   E♭7   F♭7   G♭7   A♭7   B♭♭7   C7

Using the other two minor scales, these additional chromatic seventh chords may be derived:

B♭7   C♭7

D. THE SECONDARY SUBDOMINANT CHORD AND THE SECOND-

ARY SUBDOMINANT MINOR CHORD. In the same way in which the secondary dominant seventh and the chromatic dominant seventh chords are
constructed in relationship to each of the scale tones, secondary subdominant chords and secondary subdominant minor chords may be constructed. Each of these chords has the same relationship to the tones of the
scale that the MAJ or MIN built on the fourth step of the scale has to the
Tonic. (The fourth step—IV—is called the Subdominant). The secondary
subdominant of III in the key of C major would be an A chord. The secondary subdominant minor of II in the key of C major would be a G min.
chord. Secondary subdominant chords and secondary subdominant minor
chords are notated in reference to the tone to which they are related.
This is abbreviated as IV-/III (A min. in the key of C major) and IV-/II
(G min. in the key of C minor).

The secondary subdominant chords in C major are:

G   A   B♭   C   D   E

The secondary subdominant chords in C minor are:

G   A♭   B♭   C   D♭   E

Using the other two minor scales, these additional secondary subdominant chords may be derived:

D   E♭

The secondary subdominant minor chords in C major are:

Gmin.   Amin.   B♭min.   Cmin.   Dmin.   Emin.

The secondary subdominant minor chords in C minor are:

Gmin.   A♭min.   B♭min.   Cmin.   D♭min.   Emin.

Using the other two minor scales, these additional secondary subdominant minor chords may be derived:

Dmin.   E♭min.

E.   THE SECONDARY SUPERTONIC SEVENTH CHORD. A chord
may be built above each of the scale steps of both major and minor in
the same relationship that the chord built on II has to I. In major, this
chord is called the II7 of the step to which it is related. In minor, this
chord is called the II7—of the step to which it is related. F♯min.7 would
be II7/III in the key of C major. Gmin.7(♭5) would be called II7-/IV in
the key of C minor.

The secondary supertonic seventh chords in C major are:

Emin.7   F#min.7   Gmin.7   Amin.7   Bmin.7   C#min.7

The secondary supertonic seventh chords in C minor are:

Emin.7(♭5)   Fmin.7(♭5)   Gmin.7(♭5)   Amin.7(♭5)

B♭min.7(♭5)   C#min.7(♭5)

Using the other two minor scales, these additional supertonic seventh chords may be derived:

Bmin.7(♭5)   Cmin.7(♭5)

The secondary II7- is often used in major, but the secondary II7 is not frequent in minor.

32   THE PROGRESSION OF CHORDS DERIVED FROM SCALES

A.   The most usual movement of the roots of consecutive chords is a perfect fifth down. Almost as frequent is the progression down a perfect fourth. Third most usual is the movement (up or down) of a major or minor third. (Because of the resulting common tones between chords so constructed, this movement is somewhat weak: C to Emin.7.) Not so usual, but very good, is the progression of chords built on tones a major or minor second apart.

B.   Any diatonic chord of major may progress to any other diatonic chord of major. Any diatonic chord of minor may progress to any other diatonic chord of minor.

C.   Any diatonic chord of minor may be used in the major key built on the same tone (chords extracted from E minor may be used in E major). The borrowed chords from minor are usually used in place of the corresponding major chord. For example, in C major the VI of minor may be used in place of the regular VI. This substitution would produce would produce A♭ to G7 instead of Amin.7 to G7, a refreshing change.

The reverse is also true. Chords from major may be used in the corresponding minor key.

D.   Any diatonic chord may progress to any subordinate structure (by "subordinate structure," these chords are meant: secondary dominant seventh chords, chromatic dominant seventh chords, secondary subdominant chords, secondary subdominant minor chords, and secondary supertonic seventh chords). Diatonic chords of major usually go to subordinant chords of major; diatonic chords of minor usually go to subordinate chords of minor.

E.   Subordinate chords may move freely to other subordinate chords of the same class. Secondary subdominant chords may move freely to other secondary subdominant chords, for example.

F.   Any subordinate chord may progress to any dominant seventh type chord.

G.   Any subordinate chord may progress directly to a chord built on the tone to which it is related. (A Gmin. may go to a Dmin.7 in the key of C; this is a IV/II to a II.) Secondary dominant seventh chords and chromatic dominant seventh chords are very likely to progress to a chord built on the tones to which they are related. The tendency of the chromatic seventh to resolution is especially strong.

H.   The first few and last few chords of a given harmonic progression should have a close relationship to the original key in order to preserve the sense of tonality.

The material in this chapter may be applied in these ways: (1) to harmonize a melody (one which has been previously harmonized or one without harmonies), or (2) to establish a chordal progression upon which a melody may be written.

33   MIXED VOICING

The manner in which a melodic line may be treated can be divided into three main categories: (1) as an identity (unison, octave, double octave, etc.), (2) in close position voicing (including the thickened line and the widened line), and (3) in open position voicing (using the given positions for four, five, or six voices or by voicing four or more voices without positions). The three categories may be intermixed in any way.

A.   Although the widened line is derived from close position principles, it will have a larger range. In this respect it is similar to open position. It may be combined with open position very naturally: (1) to accommodate a fast-moving figure within an otherwise sustained passage, or (2) when its parallelism is desirable, especially on a moderately percussive figure.

Open position may be combined with any form of close position: (1) to accommodate a few sustained tones within an otherwise fast-moving, parallel passage, or (2) when its interwoven texture is desirable, often as a contrast to the sweep of close position (especially the extreme parallelism of the thickened line and the widened line).

B. Identities may supplement voiced passages; voicings may not be used to supplement identities. Used with open position voicing, identities are most often assigned to prefatory, connecting figures, usually of a less sustained nature. With close position voicing, identities are most often used to facilitate a very fast-moving or particularly difficult passage. They may also be used for their greater power or for the change of color they provide.

C. In combining identities with voiced passages, the following considerations should determine whether unison, octave, or double octave should be used: (1) the distribution which lies best for the instruments in question, (2) the distribution which creates the most natural <u>connection</u> between each of the voices—from chord to identity and/or identity to chord, (3) the distribution whose <u>sound</u> best fits the context.

D.   A well-defined change from the thickened line to the widened line is an excellent coloring. Any of the forms of close position may be intermixed—usually, though, when required by circumstances:

1.   When a line goes up, widened line may be used to minimize the range of the harmony parts:

2.   When a passage goes down, widened line may be abandoned for thickened line or close position:

3.   A few notes of an harmonic nature may demand larger and more powerful chords than thickened or widened line supply:

4.   A few notes may demand the supple and facile nature of thick-

ened or widened line rather than strict or modified close position:

5. The <u>exact</u> parallelism of thickened or widened line may be required:

6. The freer bass voice of modified close position may be desirable.

It is best to switch between thickened line and widened line or between the different forms of the thickened line when the melody line makes a large skip. In this way, the lower parts continue to simulate, in modified form, the movement of the lead voice.

Extreme differences in treatment should be made only when required by the content or as a deliberate change of color. Within one segment of a composition, more than two methods of treatment should be used only when <u>demanded</u> by the passage in question.

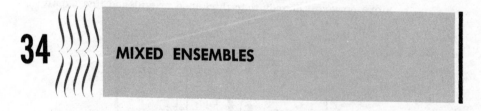

34 MIXED ENSEMBLES

It is often desirable to use a more varied line for ensemble than is permitted by the exclusive use of any of the four ensemble methods previously outlined.

Which ensemble method suits which passage? The basic ensemble technique is designed for simple passages of limited range and sustained rhythms; the four-tone ensemble is suited to rapid passages with many scales; the percussive ensemble method is designed for passages of extremely limited range, having many detached and repeated tones; the unison ensemble method is designed for passages of great range (often with large skips) and of distinctly strong melodic character.

At first it is best to mix only two of the ensemble methods within one passage. Combined use of two methods will usually cause no problems.

The content of the passage must <u>demand</u> the change of ensemble technique. In other words the mixture of techniques must not be used unless required. The only possible exception is a phrase which possesses characteristics allowing the use of more than ensemble method; if such a phrase is used twice in succession, it may be desirable to treat it in two different ways. Here, the difference of treatment is a form of development or transformation.

A change of ensemble method within a passage is best made between phrases. This makes the change easier for the player and less conspicuous to the listener. If it is not possible to change between phrases, the change should be made at separation points within the phrase—at rests, before or after accented (and detached) chords, etc.

A.   From percussive ensemble to basic ensemble or vice versa: since the saxophones function similarly in these two methods, they present little problem. There is a shift in the brass voicing, however, which is the difficulty of this mixture. (Occasional detached tones within a basic ensemble passage are better treated without change to the percussive ensemble technique.)

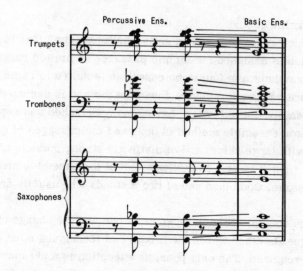

B.   From percussive or basic ensemble to the four-note ensemble: these are excellent combinations of methods. Here the distribution of the saxophones for the four-note method should be as close as possible to the last position of the saxophones for the percussive or basic ensemble. There is a tendency for the trombones to make too great a shift upward into the compactness of the four-note positions. This problem is avoided if the first few tones of the four-note ensemble are lower.

C.   From the four-note ensemble to the percussive or basic ensemble: here the problem is that the saxophones and lower trombones may be higher for the last chords of the four-note method than they are as they go into the new method. This discrepancy can be minimized if the last few chords of the four-note method are lower, allowing the lower voices to move smoothly into the new method. The shift from the narrow four-note method into the wider basic or percussive method must necessarily involve skips of some of the voices; it is better if these skips are made by the upper instruments, however.

D.   From unison ensemble to percussive or basic ensemble: the only precaution here concerns the distribution of the unison ensemble, which should allow each instrument to move easily to the first note of the new ensemble. Previous rules about the distribution of identities on ensemble should also be kept in mind.

Note, too, that the power of identities is so great that the mixture of a high register identity and either percussive or basic ensemble will be incorrectly balanced if the voiced ensembles are to be as powerful or more powerful than the identity—the voiced ensemble will have less power, even though the lead tones are the same and the parts are played with as much power.

E.   From any voiced ensemble to unison ensemble: the smooth and simple leading of each part from the voiced ensemble to the identities is not as important here as in the reversed procedure, since moving into an identity is easier than moving into a harmony part. This is so because of the firmness and binding power of the identity; stepping into a unison or octave tone is like becing carried by a strong undercurrent — the player is <u>pulled</u> into the identity.

    F.   From unison ensemble to four-note ensemble: see the first paragraph of D, above. It is often wise to thin out the unison ensemble when it is combined with the four-note ensemble. At least, the dynamics of the unison ensemble should be proportionately less. These measures are designed to compensate for the lesser strength of the four-note methods.